Phillip J. Stone

How to *NOT* Lose Friends and Fight with Other People

An Entertaining Fable about Masting Conflict, Reading Minds, and Winning with Words

Questions Are the **Answer**

Copyright ©2025 by Phillip J. Stone

ALL RIGHTS RESERVED. No part of this book may be reproduced in any form or by any electronic or mechanical means including information storage and retrieval systems without permission in writing from the author, except by a reviewer, who may quote brief passages in a review.

Design and distribution by Bublish

Published by Stone Global, LLC

ISBN: 979-8-9924732-2-3 (eBook)
ISBN: 979-8-9924732-0-9 (Paperback)
ISBN: 979-8-9924732-1-6 (Hardcover)

This fable is a work of fiction based on actual events in the author's life. The Phil Stone character is based on the author. All other characters, and the businesses mentioned, are wholly imaginary. With those characters and business names, any and all resemblances to persons living or dead, or existing businesses, is entirely coincidental.

CONTENTS

Welcome!..v
Introducing My Fictional Cast of Characters xi

Chapter 1: THE MAGIC OF CHOICES 1
Chapter 2: DECISIONS 11
Chapter 3: ACCEPTANCE................................28
Chapter 4: EVALUATION 43
Chapter 5: GO STEP-BY-STEP...........................56
Chapter 6: PERSPECTIVES 66
Chapter 7: TRANSFORMATION 83
Chapter 8: ASSUMPTIONS...............................95
Chapter 9: BENEFITS..................................108
Chapter 10: CHALLENGES 119
Chapter 11: DEVELOPMENT..............................129
Chapter 12: MIND-READING TECHNIQUES 136
Chapter 13: ELEVATION................................148
Epilogue: THE ACCIDENT...............................159

Topics for Contemplation and Discussion 163
About the Author, by Deborah Grandinetti, Editor 171

WELCOME!

Hey. Great to see you here. I'm Phillip J. Stone. Come on in. Step into my office. I've got something important to share with you.

We have a problem—a big problem. You see it everywhere. It's totally consuming. And it's spreading—like a virus. It threatens us all. What is it? Conflict!

We live on a planet with eight billion people. More is heating up than just our temperatures. More is rising than just our sea levels. More is threatening than pandemics. More! Major powers are scrambling for it—more land, more resources, more power! It's a race to control Earth's remaining resources, and solar system domination. With conflict going global, entire populations are threatened.

Conflict is everywhere. Our day-to-day interactions are filled with it. Negotiating through conflict requires patience. Knowing how to move people with easily learned persuasion and communication skills—that's your key for navigating through conflict—both the simple situations, and the complex.

If we were to make a list of predicaments leading to conflict, that list would be never-ending. And each situation needs a solution. Finding the best solutions is easy for those who have cultivated their communication and persuasion skills. Our goal here? To get you those skills—get you solutions!

Do any of the following situations sound familiar?

You get your medical bill and see your insurance company denied your claim, leaving you to pay the entire bill out of pocket. You call the insurance company and dispute their denial—conflict.

You work at a summer camp and discover one of the kids is stealing food, but their parents deny any possibility—conflict.

You think your teenager is sound asleep. You peek in their bedroom and see the empty bed and the open window—conflict.

You make a reservation at the hottest restaurant well in advance before your big celebration, but when you check in, they can't find your name on their list, and the place is packed—conflict.

You coach a sports team. One of your players fouls their opponent and the referee kicks them out of the game. You don't see it that way—conflict.

You manage a corporation and discover the people in accounting despise the salespeople—because they believe salespeople are paid far too much money—conflict.

You've been looking all over for the season's hottest gift, the one everyone has to have, and see the last one on the store shelf. As you reach to snag it, another person grabs it too—conflict.

As you go through the intersection, you see a flashing red light in your rearview mirror. You hear the sound of a police siren, and realize they are coming after you—conflict.

You are a customer service employee, or you sell things, or you work on home improvement projects, or you have a classroom filled with kids, or you collect on bad debts, or… If you are alive, it's everywhere—conflict. Some conflict is so minor, it's easily overcome. But what about really challenging circumstances? How do you get yourself out of these tough situations without losing friends and pissing off countless people?

I wrote this fable to show you how! Why a fable? To make it fun! It's a blend of fact and fiction, with solutions sprinkled throughout the story.

Imagine this. Imagine you learn to read people's minds. You'd meet a new person and instantly know who they are. Are they honest? Which way do they lean politically? Where are they on religion? You'd understand how they tick. Do they have integrity? Are they pro this? Are they anti that? And a big one—you would know what they think about you!

When you know their thoughts, you can always say the right thing. You can eliminate conflict. You will never misunderstand. If you want to make a point, you will know exactly what to say and how to say it. When you learn to read people's minds you free yourself of the worry of saying the wrong thing.

Ah! If only mind reading was possible!

Well, guess what! You *can* read people's minds. I will show you how! It's easy!

You want to know what people are thinking? Ask them! Questions are the answer. I'll prove it. The right question at the right time prompts people to open up and tell you their thoughts. The wrong question does the opposite. Do it wrong and you create conflict. Let me show you how to easily recognize the difference, so you can always choose wisely.

I've been selling forever. Believe it or not—so have you! I'll prove that to you too. When sales became my career choice, I first had to learn the actual skills needed to sell. Unlike many people, nothing comes to me automatically. I'm not a natural-born anything. God didn't program me that way. I need to clearly see the how and why of things before I can get any positive results. I first realized this shortcoming when I struggled to learn to play the guitar. Even when I reached the level of professional rock bass player, I still had to figure out why the music worked—or why it didn't, before I could master the music. When it came to my sales career, I had to learn why people would buy, and why they would not. I needed to completely understand the actual psychology behind it.

I know—it doesn't seem fair. Some people are born amazing at all kinds of things. The child prodigy. The overnight sensation. The superstar actress who was discovered in a diner. Not me. I didn't get so lucky. But there is a silver lining that came with the "curse" of always needing to understand how things work. Once I understand something, I can explain it to others! I can show people how it's done! I can teach them! Then I can coach while they work to duplicate it. That skill is a blessing—not a curse. I am so thankful!

In sales, I've won awards, fabulous trips, and big bonuses. In sales management, I have trained thousands of salespeople. I've coached hundreds of customer service professionals, and won more awards in the process. I've transformed people who opened their minds, and gave me their trust. They allowed me to lead them into the magic that comes when you read minds and eliminate conflict—by asking the right questions. It's all about the intricacies of communication.

I learned a few communication skills while raising my children too! And each of them now has children of their own. So my wife, Kim, and I get to do it all again with grandchildren. As of this writing, she and I have been married for over four decades. It was nearly fifty years ago when I began my journey into the world of persuasion. I've found communication gems with each job I've had. You know what? All those skills, from all I've done—they all intertwine! Here it is. Here you go. I've got it figured out for you!

If you are one of those people who first judge a book by jumping to the end to decide if reading it is worth your time, you are going to love this! I've listed the most powerful ideas and concepts at the very end. Check it out. Now, if you are the more patient type, you'll find these gems tucked throughout the book. The end list can serve as your review. Either way—enjoy!

In the following pages you will meet people who have become my lifelong friends, the Ross family. They have challenges like all the rest of us, but they continue to thrive. With enhanced persuasion and communication skills, they have learned how to read minds—so everyone wins! You will see exactly how they did it so you can duplicate their results!

Doug Ross is a successful career fireman. However, a major promotion finds Doug out of his comfort zone. His people are quitting and he cannot figure out why. He embraces persuasion concepts and turns things around. He elevates his game. Doug has a clear understanding of the power of questions and uses that knowledge to take his career at the Bonnerville Fire House to new heights.

His daughter, Nina Ross, embraced these methods early in her career. She learned how to avoid conflict. You will too. She overcame one obstacle after another and now enjoys a thriving career headed for stardom. As a co-mentor of Nina Ross, her string of successes made me incredibly proud. Nina has become a master at persuasion—and avoiding conflict! And she's just getting started!

There are times in life when we have to explain ourselves. There are times we demand explanations from others. My promise to you is this—no matter which side of a conversation you are on, what you will learn from this fable will illuminate your pathway to success!

INTRODUCING MY FICTIONAL CAST OF CHARACTERS

Phil Stone: That's me. Am I fictional? Not totally, depending on who you ask. I'm real. But, unlike in my real world, in Bonnerville—I get to be infallible! I interface with all the characters as a friend, coach, and mentor. Can't wait for you to join me there, in Bonnerville!

Dr. Loretta Ross: She owns and runs an optical office in the idyllic town of Bonnerville, where she offers prescription glasses. She and her staff display consummate customer service skills. She is a commanding and decisive woman who bases decisions on logic.

Douglas Ross: He is a career fireman and Dr. Loretta Ross's husband. He was recently promoted to Bonnerville Fire Chief. The transition creates inner conflict for Doug. He even questions his leadership skills. But Doug is a great student. You'll see.

Nina Ross: She is Doug and Loretta's only child. She just graduated near the top of her high school class, and has no idea what to do next. She has a passion for learning and is an amazingly quick study. Phil Stone would tell you Nina is his favorite protegee. He loves coaching her.

Jaxine Jackson: Jaxie is Nina's best friend. She is also an only child, and graduated with Nina near the top of their class. She seems to be a natural persuader and orchestrates a once-in-a-lifetime road trip with Nina across the USA. She is always there for Nina, even with

Jaxie off to college and beyond. She and Nina will forever remain inseparable.

Paul and Anne Jackson: They are Jaxie's parents. Anne is a loving wife and dedicated parent whose support of her husband knows no limits. Paul is an electrician, a diligent worker, a prudent saver, and a selfless man who saved Fred Freed at Freedom Ford.

Fred Freed: Fred pioneered the founding of Freedom Ford decades back. He knows everybody in Bonnerville. He runs his car dealership with his servant leadership style. He is loyal to all his friends, and he never forgets to put other people first.

Millie: She is the receptionist at the main hotel in Bonnerville, a quaint mid-sized town with snow-capped mountains in the distance. Everyone loves Millie. Her smile melts the hearts of every hotel guest she serves at The Bonner Hotel. Her retirement changes Nina Ross's life.

Jason Bonner: Jason is the great-grandson of Stuart Bonner, the founder of Bonnerville. His family built The Bonner Hotel. When Jason started a family, he stepped into the role of hotel manager. He practices servant leadership too. He puts the employees of The Bonner Hotel above himself when making decisions.

Tony Delvecchio: He takes over as General Manager of The Bonner Hotel. Deceit lives in his heart. His investment group and their underhanded methods destroy Bonnerville's balance.

Wayne Simonton: Wayne is the unpretentious General Manager at Allworld Insurance. His path intersects with Nina's, and his plan brings Nina Ross to a major milestone in her young career.

One last thing before we dive in. Each chapter begins with a brief summary of the key concepts you will find in that chapter—then the story. I'd like to begin by...*drum roll please*...introducing: **The Ross Family**.

CHAPTER 1

THE MAGIC OF CHOICES

> Concepts:
>
> Life is a series of never-ending choices—moment by moment, nano-second by nano-second. Picking the perfect option can be a daunting, stressful, anxiety-producing, and even debilitating activity. Life is all about choices—inescapable choices. Recognizing what choices are available, and understanding how to navigate them to get the best possible result will determine the quality of that life—your life! Take command of choices. Make magic! Here's how…

This is the story of Phil Stone and the Ross family in the captivating town of Bonnerville. Through many thought-provoking vignettes, you'll see real-life examples of how these time-tested, tried-and-true, and duplicatable mind-reading strategies work.

It all started when Phil was about to board the plane for a business trip. *"Strange,"* he thought. *"The billboard listing the departing flights looks blurry."* He blinked and shook his head. It was still blurry. *"Damn. It's my eyes! Can't believe I'm gonna' need glasses."*

There was a little eyeglass shop in Bonnerville called Fairview Eyewear. Phil had never paid it any attention. His eyesight had always been perfect. Not anymore. He stopped in to schedule an appointment. "We have an opening tomorrow at ten o'clock. Can you make that?" the receptionist at Fairview asked.

"Oh, that's awesome," Phil replied. "I will juggle things around and I'll be here at ten o'clock!" She handed him an appointment card and he left.

That next morning, Phil did his best scrambling, fighting through the stress that comes every time there are last-minute changes to a plan. Phil barely got to the Fairview door at ten o'clock. The receptionist looked up. "I made it!" Phil said triumphantly, trying to catch his breath.

There must have been twenty people sitting in the waiting room. Typical—none of them uttered a word. Phil watched out of the corner of his eye as a woman began whispering to the man next to her. Phil thought, *"It's way too quiet in here with nobody talking. And this lady feels she has to stay as quiet as possible and whisper? Why? Could it be these people are that afraid of doctors?"*

Then the receptionist looked up. Phil didn't like the look of surprise on her face. She was running her finger down her touch-screen appointment calendar when she said, "I have you here for ten o'clock tomorrow!"

"Tomorrow? Oh, nuts!" Phil pulled his appointment card from his pocket and sure enough, ten o'clock was written there, but no day or date. He thought, *"Could she have said, 'Day after tomorrow' and*

I misunderstood? I need to pay closer attention to what people say, really listen so I really understand. Oh well. No point in blurting out some snide comment I would surely regret later."

Phil tried again the next morning. He arrived at ten o'clock, stress-free. Same receptionist—same look on her face. "I apologize," she said, without a hint of sincerity. "Something came up and the Optometrist is not available today."

"Well, is there anybody else here who can take care of me?" Phil asked.

"No," she said rather bluntly. She ran her finger down the appointment calendar and said, "I'll put you in for our very first appointment of the day next Tuesday at eight o'clock. That work?"

Two times Phil had been disappointed. He remembered what his friend taught him. "If something negative happens one time, it's an event. There is no point trying to develop an elaborate solution. The same situation may never reoccur. But if it happens over and over, it's a trend. If you recognize a negative trend, you must change something or be cursed to deal with that same negative again and again."

Phil decided to call Fairview Eyewear to confirm his third appointment. No last-minute surprises this time.

"Mr. Stone, I was about to call you," the receptionist said. "We have a scheduling problem tomorrow. Can you make it at one o'clock Wednesday? Eight o'clock tomorrow just won't work."

Yep. It was not an event—it was a trend—a negative trend. Three times they scheduled an appointment for Phil, and three times they failed to keep those appointments—and with no sincere apology! It was the epitome of miserable customer service. Phil knew she could hear irritation in his voice when he said, "Nope. I will have to call you back." Fairview pissed Phil off and lost him as a client, and lost him as a friend. He was done with them!

Squinting as he drove home, Phil stopped at a blurry red traffic light and took out his phone. He typed "Optical businesses around me" into his maps app. One came up just a few miles away. It was New Vision Optical, run by Dr. Ross.

Her website looked professional, and her reviews were five-star, so Phil called to schedule an appointment with Dr. Ross. All he was looking for was new glasses, but what he found was life changing. Thanks to Dr. Ross, he developed a crystal-clear understanding of the power of alternate of choice questions, a persuasion strategy where someone offers no more than two choices at one time, where either choice is a win for the person offering those two choices. Alternate of choice is a great way to nudge people toward "yes" and away from "no."

But going to New Vision brought more than new glasses and a refresher on alternate of choice—it brought Phil to Doug.

On the day of his appointment, after only a few minutes in the reception room, Phil found himself seated behind an elaborate, but intimidating machine. A professional-looking woman dressed in doctor's white approached and said, "I'm Doctor Ross. Relax. We will take care of everything." Her voice was calming, and at the same time, very confident and official sounding. While reviewing the questionnaire Phil had filled out, she asked him health and vision questions, just as he would have expected. She kept it conversational—comfortable. Then she found a pathway leading right to Phil's heart. She asked about his family. That was smart. It showed she cared about more than her practice. She cared about Phil, the person, not just some patient! Her relaxed, confident demeanor took away all the typical stress a patient can feel in a doctor's office.

The machine had multiple interchangeable lenses. Dr. Ross evaluated one eye at a time. She had Phil look through one lens, and then she switched to the next lens. "Is this one good or was the first one better?" she asked. One after another, she had him choose the better of two lenses.

Minutes later she declared, "We've got it!" Then she directed him to the frame room to pick out the frames for his glasses. The frame room was about twelve feet wide by the same twelve feet deep with racks filled with frames on every wall—even on the back of the door. Phil stood there alone, completely overwhelmed. There were hundreds of frames, and if you've ever bought prescription glasses, you know they are not cheap, and you can't return them. Phil was afraid of making a choice he might regret later. Fear of making a mistake was crippling his decision-making capability. Phil stood there thinking, "*This should be easy. Should be—but it's not!*"

Finally, Dr. Ross came in. She asked, "Find something yet?"

"You're kidding, right? I have no idea where to even start."

But as she had done determining Phil's prescription, she used alternate of choice questions again. With the right questions—she did make it easy. "Don't worry," she said. "First, the frames on these two walls are for women." That eliminated half of the frames in the room. Then Dr. Ross picked up a black plastic frame and a wire-rimmed frame. She asked, "Which of these two do you like best?" It was another alternate of choice question.

Phil pointed to the wire-rimmed frames. That eliminated almost half of the men's frames. She put away the dark plastic framed glasses and picked up another of the wire framed. "Do you like the big aviator style, or the smaller more contemporary frames?"

He picked the smaller of the two.

"Gold or silver?" she asked.

He picked gold.

"Half-wire or this with the wire that goes all the way around each lens?"

He selected the half-wire.

She picked up two gold half-wire frames designed for smaller lenses and said, "We've narrowed it down to these two. Which one do you prefer?"

Phil was amazed. Through a series of alternate of choice questions, Dr. Ross had eliminated every frame in the room, except for two. "That was a lot easier than I thought," he said. "You have hundreds of choices here. Now my problem is just deciding between these two."

With infectious excitement in her voice she said, "Actually we have over six-hundred frames here, and I've got a suggestion for you. You could get just one of these…or…you get both frames! We'll make one clear, and the other we'll make into sunglasses. You want just one, or do you like the idea of one clear and another sunglasses?"

Phil smiled and said, "I'll take them both! Sold!"

Phil stood there letting his mind replay what had just happened. In less than thirty minutes he had been signed in, examined, and led to select two great pairs of glasses. Suddenly he heard whispering. "Hey babe? Retti? You there?" The voice was coming from just outside the frame room door.

"Just me in here," Phil answered.

A tall man about six-feet-two with the build of an athlete, peered around the door. He was Phil's size and stature, but years younger. "I'm looking for my wife," the guy said.

"Aside from the Doctor, it's been just me in here," Phil answered.

This man had a rare gift. His smile lit the room. Phil instantly liked him. His warmth made the uncomfortable moment of meeting a stranger disappear as he explained, "Loretta is my wife—Retti for short. Sorry if I startled you."

"No. All good," Phil said, as he reached to shake the hand of this obviously cool guy. "I have to tell you. This office and the Doctor here are amazing. You know Fairview Eyewear?" The guy nodded. "Fairview irritated me. Then I found this place. Here, they set my appointment without making me feel like a criminal being interrogated, firing one question after another at me. I got here on time. I filled out a simple questionnaire, and as soon as I got done, they got me in."

This guy seemed genuinely intrigued. Showing sincere interest was a great way to quickly endear himself, and make a memorable first impression. He made Phil smile again. Then Phil asked, "Let me guess. Your wife—Loretta. She must work here, right?"

The guy chuckled. "Well, actually she does. I'm Douglas Ross. My wife is Dr. Ross. Call me Doug. Call her Loretta, she won't mind at all."

It suddenly made sense. Phil blurted out, "Ross! Doug Ross! You're the doctor's husband? Doctor Ross is Loretta Ross! Boy, I feel kinda' stupid. Well great to meet you, Doug. I'm Phil Stone. And the doctor, your wife…what did you call her?"

"Retti," he said. "When we first met, her little sister couldn't pronounce Loretta. I thought it sounded so adorable; I started calling her Retti too. Don't think she liked it at first. You know, someone's name is precious. She thought 'Retti' sounded too much like 'ready.' It does, I guess. But it stuck—and she's great with it now—after all our years together."

"Retti? I like that," Phil said. "And you are right about a person's name. I remember being introduced to Pantelis Hatziprontos. I was told I could call him Peter. He didn't offer that himself—the introducer did."

"Really? That's a tough name. How did he take it—being called Peter?" Doug asked.

"He didn't seem to mind. He knows his name is a challenge for people. Phil Stone—who could mess that up—but Pantelis Hatziprontos? That could easily be mispronounced."

Doug shrugged his shoulders. "So, he has a tough name. Oh well. All the more reason to put in the effort and get his name right."

"I agree one hundred percent," Phil said. "After the person who introduced us went on her way, I asked him to repeat his full name."

"It's Pantelis Hatziprontos," he told Phil.

"Well great to meet you, Pantelis. And your last name, Pantelis, could you spell that for me?"

Again, showing genuine interest, Doug asked, "And was he put off by all your fussing with his name?"

"Totally the opposite—he overflowed with appreciation," Phil explained. "He spelled his last name and I finally got it exactly right. He loved the effort I was putting in. I repeated it over and over in my mind so I wouldn't lose it. I've always needed to make an extra effort to remember people's names. Everybody should. When you talk with people, use their name. Say their name to get their attention. Say their name to endear yourself to them. Always remember, a person's name is absolutely the most precious word in the world to them. I'd see the guy everybody else called 'Peter,' and I'd say, 'Hey, Pantelis Hatziprontos!' The huge smile I got back every time proved I was on to something."

Doug said, "You know, Phil…I like the way you think!"

"Well Doctor R…I mean, Loretta. She helped me sift through six hundred choices to find the perfect glasses. I've used this technique myself before, but hers was the most impressive use of 'Alternate of Choice' I have ever seen. There is a lot of magic hidden in choices."

With a quizzical look on Doug's face, he said only, "Alternate of Choice?"

"Ah. Sorry. That's a sales term—Alternate of Choice."

Doug's eyebrows went up as he grinned and said, "You must be in sales. I'm not much of a salesman. But I've always wished I was better at it. Go ahead. Tell me more."

Phil grinned too. "You give people too many choices and it can overwhelm them. They can't even think straight. We call it 'paralysis from analysis.' Exactly how I felt standing there in the frame room. Too many choices!"

"I get it," Doug said. "If you've never bought glasses before, you could get lost in that frame room. It can be bewildering in there. So how does this alternate of choice thing actually work?"

"Let me explain, Doug. An alternate of choice question offers two options. Either choice works. If I were selling books, and I ask a 'yes or no' question like, 'Do you want to buy my book?' I could get a 'no' response. If I ask an alternate of choice question like, 'Would you like one book, or two?' I'll gladly accept either choice. There's no guarantee I won't get a 'no,' but I've led you away from that 'no' and toward getting either one or two books. If you hadn't decided, my alternate of choice question could nudge you toward a book purchase.

"Doctor Loretta never gave me more than two things at a time to choose from. She did that to develop my prescription, and she did it again in the frame room. When she got me all the way to the final choice, she offered me an option I had not considered. The process was so seamless, so comfortable. It made me feel I could really trust her. So, when she suggested I get two pairs, one clear and one sunglass lenses, I said, 'Sure,' and got them both. Think about this from a sales perspective. I came to buy one pair of glasses, and I'm leaving having bought two. That's upselling. But that's another story. Point is, her use of Alternate of Choice was brilliant."

"Makes total sense," Doug said, smiling, nodding his head. "Sounds like you aggressively study this stuff. You do, don't you, Phil?"

"That's me. I consider myself a student of the art of persuasion. And I love the topic. I love to teach people how their entire life, and the lives of everyone they touch, will benefit—if they choose to master persuasion techniques. All people—not just salespeople. Teachers, coaches, managers, entrepreneurs, and anyone in customer service—anyone who interacts with others can radically improve their world and comfortably move people to their way of thinking—if they master persuasion strategies. People who call themselves salespeople but use pressure and scare tactics to sell—they just piss people off. Agree?"

"For sure."

Just then, a voice came over the intercom. "Mr. Stone. Please come to the fitting counter. Your glasses are lonely and they want you to try them on."

"Hey Doug—gotta' run. I've got lonely glasses!" Phil couldn't help but laugh. "I've enjoyed talking with you. Really, I have. Tell you what. You ever want to learn how some of this persuasion stuff works, give me a call." Phil reached out to shake Doug's hand and added, "Your wife has a whole file on me, but here's my cell number."

Phil gave Doug his card and got the final fitting for his two new pairs of eyeglasses. All the drive home he thought about the experience. He and Doug hit it off right away. And his wife and her staff did a fabulous job helping Phil. They helped him relax by skillfully handling everything he needed. He actually had fun! It was a great lesson in customer service—but it was so much more. Phil met a new friend! Phil made himself a promise to stay in touch with Doug. It proved to be a promise easily kept.

Tips from the Communication Toolbox

- *A reoccurring negative will likely happen again. Develop a plan to stop it. If a negative happens once—don't overact. Watch. It may just be a one-time event—no plan needed yet. Be aware of events and trends.*
- *When poor communication leads to misunderstandings, conflict is born.*
- *Be obvious about showing interest—in the other person, and the things that interest them.*
- *A person's name is the most precious word in their world. Use their name. Remember it.*

CHAPTER 2

DECISIONS

Concepts:

When choices are offered, decisions come next. When your choice proves to be the most perfect option—you win! Bask in the glow of success! But, when you choose poorly, you get pain. "How did I let this happen? How did I miss? How could I be so wrong? And now, how do I explain myself? What a mess I made!"

Understanding how to dissect a situation and see all the obvious options, and the hidden agendas, gives us power—the power to make that perfect decision. Having targeted tools will multiply your chances of success. Let's look at tools and strategies that greatly increase the odds of making winning decisions.

Weeks later Phil had his follow-up appointment with Dr. Ross. Instead of feeling apprehensive about a doctor visit, he looked forward to telling her how much he appreciated the way she and her staff had cared for him. While sitting in the waiting room, Phil looked up, and there he was again—Doug. Phil jumped up and extended his hand. "Hey my friend. Great to see you!"

As they shook hands Doug said, "I want to introduce you to my number one daughter, Nina."

Standing behind him was a lovely young woman who obviously was related to Doug and Loretta. They both were sharp-looking people. Nina was a blend of the two of them.

Doug stepped aside. Nina smiled and reached to shake Phil's hand. "Good to meet you, sir," she said.

"You too, and call me Phil," he replied. "So, you are number one—numero uno?"

Nina grinned and said, "Not tough when you're an only child."

Then Phil looked at Doug. "You, my friend, are a lucky man!"

"Absolutely! You're right," Doug said proudly, as he pulled Nina toward him for a daddy hug. "I'm a lucky guy."

Then Phil asked, "So how is it you are here in the middle of the morning when most folks are out there working?"

"I'm a fireman," he said.

"Really? Local?" Phil asked.

"Fire Rescue Master Station!" Doug said, gushing with pride.

"Wow. Good for you! How long have you been at it?"

"Loretta and I met in college. I had planned to go into medicine too, but … I don't know … something pulled in another direction and I've been here now for twenty-five years."

Phil smiled. "Bet you had a major 'what now' moment. Amazing how many major 'what now' moments life puts in front of us. Why? I don't know. I figure they must be crossroads for us to navigate—to learn from—and often we totally change direction. You certainly did."

Doug tugged at his chin as he said, "I can think of all kinds of 'what now' moments people have. A car accident—what now? A divorce—what now? Getting fired—what now? Even hitting the lottery numbers—what now? Don't know if I can pinpoint mine though."

"Understandable," Phil replied. "With the minor, routine things we go through every day, we run on autopilot. We wake up in the morning. What now? We don't struggle to find the answer. We do what we always do, out of habit. We drop the key fob as we get in the car. What now? Without any thought, we just pick up the fob. But if that fob slips out of our hand and falls down the storm drain, well out of reach, we have a major 'what now' moment! We will have to devote serious thought and effort to retrieve that fob. We need the solution!"

Doug said, "I never thought about it that way. Every moment has a 'what now.' I admit, there have been times when I faced a major issue and pulled the trigger on a solution before thinking it through. If it's a big issue, it needs a big solution, one that fits. I go too fast sometimes and wind up offending somebody—or even pissing off a bunch of people. I get it."

"Ya' know, Doug. When someone is in the middle of a major 'what now,' in their mind it's a crisis, and they are out of their comfort zone. They can get so deeply involved with their crisis, they don't see the outside world. They are inwardly consumed. You've heard people talking about thinking 'outside the box,' right?"

"Sure," Doug said.

"If you allow yourself to stay inwardly consumed, you miss options. You limit your view. You're not outside the box. You're in it!"

Doug nodded. "In other words, don't overthink."

"Right," Phil said. "And don't underthink either. If we find ourselves in one of those major 'what now' moments, we need to balance the effort we put in with the severity of the situation. We don't want to drop that fob in the storm drain and walk home spending days researching the best way to retrieve it. We need a quick solution. It's about balance. My mom would have said, 'Don't make a mountain out of a molehill.'

"When it comes to 'what now' moments, you can't prepare for everything, so people need to learn to be flexible. They need to take a deep breath and weigh options before moving too fast. You were in medicine and became a fireman—quite a change of direction. So, what was behind that?"

Doug shook his head. "I guess my first major 'what now' was in biology lab where they had us dissecting rats. I never told anybody, but I came real close to throwing up. Too much blood and yuck cutting into bodies—and I hate rats. That didn't help. My second 'what now' was taking the final exam and failing. I heard they were interviewing at Master Station so I jumped ship as soon as I graduated."

Phil asked, "Any regrets?"

"Not really," Doug replied. But Phil could see regret all over Doug's face. Doug took a deep breath and admitted, "I didn't think it through. Wish I had taken my time and really weighed my options. Look at Retti. She's an optometrist. She doesn't cut into anybody. Lots of people in medicine don't deal with blood and yuck! I was too impulsive. But after twenty-five years, firefighting is in my blood now, I guess. I am a proud fireman! And I just got a huge promotion, so you won't see me here during the week much anymore. I am now the Fire Chief! I don't normally blow my own horn, but I am all fired up—excuse the pun."

"That's great, Doug. Good for you."

As Phil drove home, he thought, "*I like those people. I was blown away by Dr. Ross and her New Vision team. Then I met Doug. And now, Nina, such a poised young woman, I have obviously stumbled onto a dynamic magnetic family. Good people are a rarity—hard to find. Surround yourself with good people and good things will follow. I'll make sure to stay connected and learn more about all of them!*"

High school graduation was different for Nina. First was kindergarten, then grade school and high school—but what now? Some of her friends were going to college. Others were writing resumes and scouring the web for interview opportunities, hoping to launch their careers. A couple of them had enlisted in the armed forces. Nina figured they must like the idea of serving their beloved country. Maybe they wanted the great benefits and the pension if they made a career out of it. She decided to ask them, examining her own options, looking for insight. Instead of insight, they made her laugh. They just told her they were confused one day and found themselves in the auditorium listening to a smooth recruiter. The next thing they knew they were getting haircuts in boot camp!

"I'm taking the summer off before getting totally absorbed in college. I need a break!" Jaxie proudly announced, as she sat with Nina in the Soothie-Smoothie shop downtown.

Nina shook her head, more teasing than serious. "Here you go again," she said. "I stay home and you are off to see the world. My parents told me if I wasn't going to college this coming fall, I'd better get a job. Both of them graduated college, ya' know. The pressure is on me."

Jaxine Jackson, Jaxie for short, was the only child of Paul and Anne Jackson. Paul got his first job right out of high school as an apprentice electrician. He was a frugal saver. He and Anne had struggled for the first years of their marriage. They had money problems. They had fertility issues too. But with a little help from their parents, and dipping into their savings, they pulled through their money issues. Then they were blessed with Jaxine Elizabeth Jackson. Most young families have an even tougher time financially with a baby in the house, but Paul took on another job. He worked two jobs for years, and with his regimen of saving something every week all those years, no matter how small an amount, he and Anne could splurge on an occasional elaborate vacation. When Nina stayed home for Christmas, Jaxie was off to Europe with Paul and Anne. But Nina wasn't at all jealous of Jaxie. They were true best friends. Jaxie and Nina were at the top of the graduating class from Bonnerville High, and were highly respected by both faculty and students.

"I'm starting by renting a small RV and we'll hit the road," Jaxie announced. "We're going to visit USA parks—the big ones—the ones you and I always talk about seeing one day. Look at my plan." Jaxie opened her notepad and showed the route she had been working on. It even included a visit to Denali National Park in Alaska, a destination Nina had prayed to see one day. Jaxie made it sound incredible. "I've been working on this plan for a couple months now, and it's going to be amazing. You know what Professor Magle says at least once a day…"

"Yeah. Plan your work, and then work your plan. Sounds like you've planned a trip of a lifetime. Now you've got that plan, it's time to work it! I'm so excited for you. You said, 'We.' Who is going with you?" Nina asked.

"You!" Jaxie gushed. "Oh, Nina. I won't go without you. You need to come with me. We need to go together. It would be perfect. Oh, Nina—please? I am counting on you!"

Shaking her head, Nina felt like she was being pulled in two directions. "I wish. I wish I could. How am I supposed to convince my mom and dad? I love the idea. I wish I could."

Jaxie got excited. "So, you are in if we can get your parents blessing? We convince them and you're good? That's all? We can do that! Get your parents onboard and it's a road trip!" Nina nodded. Jaxie stood up from their table and started to pace back and forth. "Okay. Let's figure this out. Who told you college or a job—your mom or dad?"

"Mom."

"Hmm. Mom. What about your dad? What did he say?" Jaxie asked, excitement building in her voice.

"Nothing. It was all Mom's show, come to think of it. You know, my dad is usually the guy with the stiff rules. Now that he's been promoted to chief, he's a little stressed. But for me and the job thing? He didn't seem to care."

"Think you could convince your dad? We sell him on our road trip—and then if we can get him to help us sell your mom, we're golden."

"Ah. You know. He's tough," Nina complained. She was struggling, trying to conjure up some kind of plan that would open her dad up to the road trip idea. She smiled and said, "But he likes you! Maybe I can ask him in front of you? Ya' think?"

Jaxie nodded and grinned. "Grab your phone. Take some notes. Let's find an angle we can go with. We need a pathway that will get your dad to agree to our road trip plan. Remember the story of how Ben Franklin made decisions?"

"Who?"

"Ben Franklin. The old guy on hundred-dollar bills. That's why we call a hundred a 'Benjamin,' right?"

"Oh, yeah. Right. So go ahead. Tell me," Nina said.

"You should remember. Professor Magle told the story in class. How'd you space it?" Nina shrugged her shoulders as Jaxie went on with the story. "When Ben had a tough thing to solve, he'd tear a page from his notebook and fold it vertically in half. That divided the paper into two columns. At the top of the left column he would write the words, 'Reasons Against,' and top right he would put 'Reasons For.' Then he'd think through the quandary. He'd write down all the reasons he could foresee—plus and minus, and when he could think of no more, he'd tally them up. If he found more reasons for than against, he'd see that as a positive and would take that direction. If there were more reasons against, he would drop the idea. We could use that to help get this decision made, don't ya' think?"

Nina smiled. "I don't need to write some dumb list—won't help me. I can think of a thousand reasons to go, and only one reason not to: my parents!"

"No. That's not what I mean. We need to figure out what your dad might write down if he were making his own list. We can use the Ben Franklin method to brainstorm ways to convince your dad. We're kind of guessing at what he would think. Then we can formulate a plan to sell him on our trip. Like that idea?"

"Okay," Nina replied, skeptically.

Jaxie warned, "And you can't say your parents are a reason against going. We need to get specific. For example, one negative your dad could write down is money. What else?"

Thinking hard, Nina offered, "I won't be around to help out at the house." She paused and then thought of another. "My car will be just sitting. They are gonna' have to start it so the battery doesn't die. They might have to move it around too. It could be in the way."

"What else? There must be more," Jaxie prodded.

"Like what? I can't think of anything."

"Okay. It's not much of a list, but we can certainly go with these. Looks like it boils down to only three objections your dad could have—three we have thought of anyway: money, you not being around to help, and dealing with your car. Let's go over how we can handle each of these. While we're at it, list some 'reasons for.'" Jaxie sat thinking for a minute, and said, "Let's start with the biggest negative: money."

Again standing up and pacing back and forth, Jaxie continued. "My parents are covering the cost of the RV rental as part of my graduation present. No worries there. I know you've got savings. Can you tap into that a little?" she probed.

"Ha. Won't need to. I got buckets of cash and gift cards from everybody for graduation. I still can't believe it—more than I could need for our trip. I'm good!"

Jaxie clapped her hands together and said, "Awesome. If we can split gas and food, I can even cover RV Parks costs. The RV I picked sleeps four, so the two of us will be plenty comfy. That should solve the 'money.' RV parks with electricity and showers are scheduled for our every stop. And I researched and picked only ones known for being safe and secure."

Nina put her hand up to interrupt. "Security. That's another 'reason against' I think. We'll have to prove that to my dad."

"Good point. I'll put each park's security ratings and info into the plan I have written in my notebook, so when I show him the plan, he'll see how much thought we put into safety for us," Jaxie said as she sat back down and took a sip of her smoothie. "Now, what about stuff you do around the house?"

"I have things I'm expected to do—chores." Nina's face strained in concentration, but suddenly she started to laugh. "I'm being crazy. They won't have to buy food for me. One of my chores is doing my laundry. Ha. I won't be here. No laundry. No dirty dishes from me. No messes on the dining table. No bed to make. I won't be in it. Me not being here can be spun as a total positive. Let's move that to the 'reasons for' side. We got that one covered."

Jaxie asked, "Didn't your parents get your Sweet Sixteen Mustang at Freedom Ford?"

"Yeah, why?"

"Paul, my dad, is a good friend of Fred Freed. Mr. Freed owns the place. My dad did electrical work at Freedom years ago. He swears by Freedom Ford. Every new car he gets is from Freedom. When our family went to Europe over vacation, Dad had his car serviced and then stored at Freedom. I'm sure I can get Dad to work that out for you. Heck—your dad bought your Mustang at Freedom. They service it for you anyway. Should be easy. Hey—let me try him now. I'll catch my dad on his cell."

Jaxie picked up her phone and said, "Hey Siri. Call Paul Jackson."

"Hey Jaxie," Paul said, as his daughter's voice came over his car audio. "What's up?"

"I need a favor, Daddy. Nina and I are working through my road trip plan, and the only obstacle is her car. Do you think you could get Mr. Freed to store her car like he did for you over Christmas?"

Paul wasn't sure. He said, "That's a long time—all summer. Hmm. Let me give Fred a shout. I'll call you right back."

Fred Freed did exhaustive research before setting up Freedom Ford decades ago. As he mapped out his plan, he remembered the cute joke he heard years earlier that supposedly came from the late 1800's when countless people set off to go west. "How do you tell the difference between a pioneer and a settler?" the joke began. "The settler is the guy with the plow in his hands. The pioneer is the guy with the arrows in his back." Fred needed to avoid the arrows that threaten all pioneers. And arrows there were. The worst was Fred's opening day at Freedom Ford.

He had a huge Grand Opening Event planned—lots of time and money invested, and it was Paul Jackson who found the electrical issue that was about to kill that event. Paul Jackson saved the day for Freedom Ford, and Fred Freed was eternally grateful.

"Hey Paul. How are you?" Fred said as he picked up the call.

"Listen. Hate to be a bother, but I've got a really big favor to ask. And you tell me if I'm going too far. I don't want to take advantage—just because I helped you a long time back."

Fred was curious, but concerned. Paul was making this sound like something monumental. "I'll do what I can for you. You know that. So, what's up?"

"My daughter, Jaxie, is best friends with Nina Ross. You know Nina? Doug Ross's daughter?"

"Sure. They got her Mustang here," Fred replied, as he tried to figure out what was on Paul's mind.

Paul explained, "The girls are planning a road trip this summer. Big obstacle is Nina's car. Would it be asking too much of you—could I ask you to store her Mustang while she and Jaxie visit our national parks? Am I going too far?"

By the way Paul was talking, Fred was expecting to be asked a huge favor. He was bracing for it. But this was easy. "That's all? No problem! None. I'll keep it in the back. For you, Paul—anything!"

Paul called Jaxie right back. He said, "Done deal, honey. Fred's a great guy. No problem at all. Just call him when you're ready and he'll take care of everything!"

Jaxie smiled at Nina and said, "I knew Dad could work magic with Freedom Ford. All set!"

"You're the best, Jaxie. I can picture cruising down the highways in that RV now. I need to think about packing, don't I? Wait. Let me ask—when do think I should run this by my dad?"

Jaxie's stylus tapped on her notebook. A moment later she said, "Let's pick the day of the week and a time when he's most relaxed. You don't get positive decisions from somebody who's stressed out. Imagine trying to ask your dad to say 'yes' to our road trip when he's on his way to the dentist." Jaxie laughed. "Gotta' get him when he's relaxed."

Nina was beginning to believe. Jaxie could hear it in her voice. Nina grinned and said, "Makes sense. He used to be on three days and off the next three. Now, as chief, he's Monday through Friday almost every week. His most calm time…hmm. I'd say Saturday, late afternoon, after chores and shopping and stuff, and before my parents get into their evening. I'd say four o'clock."

"Sounds like we will be hanging out at your place Saturday afternoon," Jaxie said as they high-fived each other.

That Saturday the garage door opened and Doug walked in. There on the family room couch were Nina and Jaxie. "Hey ladies. Enjoying your Saturday?" The girls smiled back.

As Doug walked to the kitchen, out of earshot of the girls, Jaxie whispered, "Nina. Relax. Let's open a conversation with your dad before we hit him with the road trip idea. Let's let him settle in first and we can probe a little to see if we believe this is still the best time to lay this all out for him, okay?"

Nina was getting excited. She said, "How 'bout this? I'll turn the TV on and find some live sports and when Dad comes in, I can chat with him—get him relaxed."

"Yeah. Sounds good. Find sports on network TV," Jaxie suggested.

Nina didn't get it. "Huh?" she said. "Okay. Here we go. Channel four. Why network TV? Why not just stream?"

Jaxie gave her a look of astonishment. "Come on. You know. The commercials! They have commercials. We can mute the sound and talk with your dad!"

Nina laughed. "You're too much! You're not taking any chances."

The sound of a beer can cracking open signaled Doug was on his way back to the family room. He nestled down into the lounge chair and said, "Baseball. Cool."

Jaxie winked at Nina as she said, "How's your day goin' Mr. Ross?"

"Great, Jaxie. Got my honey-do list done and I'm good."

"Honeydew list? Melons?" Jaxie questioned.

Doug smiled. "No. You know. Honey do this, and honey do that, and honey, you forgot to do the other thing. My honey-do list."

Jaxie giggled and smiled back. A few minutes passed with only the sound of the sports announcer. Then the TV went to commercial. Jaxie hit the mute button and said, "We're just hanging out and doing some planning. You?"

"Planning. I like the sound of that!" Doug said. "What y'all planning?"

Leaving out all details, Jaxie said only, "Our summer."

"You gettin' a job this summer before school in the fall, Jaxie?" Doug asked.

"You know, Mr. Ross, I've been wanting to visit our national parks since I was little. My family took me to a couple, but my folks are all about Europe. I get that, but I'm all USA. I've figured out a plan to visit some of our major parks this summer. It will be a trip of a lifetime," Jaxie answered, her excitement flowing like a river. "I'll experience things and see sights that pictures or a video stream can never deliver. I'm so excited."

"Sounds amazing," Doug admitted.

Nina sat there on pins and needles as Jaxie worked magic, convincing Doug with one thought at a time as she continued her casual questions. Jaxie was methodically moving Doug to be ready for the big question. His curiosity was up. He seemed relaxed. How would Jaxie wrap this up? Nina couldn't wait to see.

Just then Jaxie got up, walked over, and opened her notebook. "Look at the plan we've got," she said.

Doug poured over the entire plan. "Ah. You pick up this RV in ten days and you're off. I like the notes and info here about each RV park and their security. You're being careful. That's critical. Good for you. And you're gone for three months? Sounds like the summer all high school grads would die for!"

Nina could tell that her dad was at least intrigued. The game came back on, but he didn't grab the remote and hit the sound—good sign.

Jaxie answered, "Yeah. I think it is great for students who really applied themselves to be rewarded. You know—to have a chance to see and do things—have new experiences and clear their heads at the same time. You agree, Mr. Ross?"

"Sure do," Doug replied enthusiastically. "And you are at the top of your class, academically, right? You deserve it!"

"Yeah. I'm proud! I ended fifth in my graduating class, right behind Nina."

Nina could feel a grin growing on her face that she didn't want her dad to see. Watching Jaxie move her dad step by step closer to saying yes when the road trip question was asked, Nina was learning powerful new ways of convincing someone. Maybe she was witnessing genius. Whatever it was—it was incredibly exciting!

Doug stood up, crunched his empty can, and as he walked back to the kitchen, he said, "We are so proud of Nina. Both of you—proud of you both."

When he returned, new beer in hand, Jaxie said, "Yeah. Nina and I had a great senior year. I even talked with Nina about coming with me on my road trip, but we couldn't figure out how to make it work."

"Oh?" Doug said. "Too bad."

"Yeah. We figured the cost wouldn't be much of an issue. My folks are covering the RV rental so it's really just meals, park fees, gas, and any entrance tickets and stuff. Nina said she got lots of graduation money, more than she could need on this trip. But we couldn't figure out how to deal with her Mustang."

"The Mustang. Right. We can't have it just sitting here for months. Smart of you to figure that one out," Doug said.

"Well, I told my dad about Nina's Mustang and he said he would do me a favor. He said with me away, the house would be quiet. The food bills would drop. There would be no Jaxie laundry. He told me they would enjoy the privacy with his little girl on a safe trip in the United

States, seeing things she might never have. My dad said he'd get Fred Freed to take care of Nina's Mustang while we are gone."

"Your dad knows Fred Freed from Freedom Ford? Me too. Bought Nina's car there. He'd take care of her car. What would that cost?" Doug asked, showing genuine interest for the first time.

"My dad said if Nina brings it in for service—any service, he could keep it in the service building with cars waiting to be picked up. No time limit for my dad, I guess, and no cost. Paul and Fred Freed go way back. Nina could just pay for an oil change. That work?" Jaxie asked.

Doug stood up and said, "Nina." There was a strong commanding tone to his voice. "Would you want to go with Jaxie?"

"Oh Dad, could I?"

"Jaxie's right," Doug answered. "This would be an awesome experience for you two. You'd see new places and fall even deeper in love with this glorious country of ours. I like it. The car would have been a problem, but looks like you guys got that figured out. And it's no money out of my pocket. Sounds exciting to me, but you know the problem, right, Nina?"

"Yep. Mom."

"We sat here last week and Retti was adamant about you either enrolling in college or getting a full-time job," Doug reminded Nina.

Nina's enthusiasm got the best of her, and she blurted out, "But we didn't talk about summer!"

Doug got stern. "Nina! I don't want this to turn into a battle."

"I'm sorry," Nina said. "I didn't mean to push."

Jaxie sat there watching silently. Moments passed. Then Doug said, "Tell you what. If you line up a job for the fall, I'll convince your mom about your summer road trip. I think it's a fabulous plan."

Doug sat there thinking, TV still on mute. Then he said, "You guys planned this all out, didn't you? Jaxie, you could have just asked me if Nina could go with you flat out. I might have said, 'no,' so you broke it down. Smart. I'll bet you guys figured out what I might object to and you came at me with those solutions. Pretty cagy."

Nina was about to apologize. Doug could see it coming and jumped in. "Don't get me wrong. I applaud your efforts. You convinced me without any pressure. If you pressured me, you know how that would have turned out. Push too hard and I'd get pissed off and there would be no road trip.

"You wanted to convince me to say 'yes' to your road trip. So, instead of asking a point-blank question like, 'Can Nina and I go on a road trip for the whole summer?' you broke it down. You asked simple little questions to see what I was thinking, and then you directed my thoughts and boosted my interest and curiosity. Very smooth! Good job ladies."

Both Nina and Jaxie had smiles plastered on their faces as Nina asked, "Dad, do you think Mom will agree? You sure?"

"Absolutely. You ladies sold me. I'll use the same approach with Mom. Instead of hitting her with a point-blank question, I'll break it down too."

That following Monday Doug knocked softly on Nina's bedroom door. "Come on in."

His head hanging down and with an apologetic look in his eyes, Doug said, "I'm sorry, honey. I blew it."

Nina was taken by surprise. "What, Dad? What happened?"

"I was excited and didn't pick a good time, I guess. I tried to ask little questions, breaking the idea down into small bites. What she was thinking—I am not sure. She seemed like she wasn't paying attention. Then, out of nowhere, she told me we had taken a position. As parents, we would be sending a bad message if we just gave in and reversed our stance. She said no. It's college or get a job, period!"

Nina was heartbroken. She sat silently on the edge of her bed, like a wilting flower. As Doug held Nina's hand in his, he said, "I know you are disappointed. Jaxie will be too. My bad. Hope you guys will forgive me."

"I forgive you, Dad. I love you." Nina had stifled her tears, but still had a pained frown on her face. "What went wrong? You were so confident."

"I can see you are upset, honey. I understand. Hate to see that look on your face. Can you do something for me? Let's try that trick Retti came up with when you were little."

"What trick?"

"You remember. When you'd get upset and had a permanent frown chiseled into your face, Mom would say, 'Give me a smile, Nina.' Remember that?" Doug asked.

"Yeah. She would tell me a smile on my face made the unhappy go away," Nina replied, sniffling as she talked. "It worked when I got cranky over nothing, but this is my summer. My trip of a lifetime—over," Nina replied, pain still showing on her face and obvious in her voice.

"I am truly so sorry, honey," Doug said. "After thinking over how it went, I picked a bad time with Retti. She was looking in the mirror, putting on her makeup, getting ready for work. Her mind must have been preoccupied. Her curt response was totally unexpected. It seemed like just an automatic conditioned response."

"Conditioned response?" Nina asked.

Doug painted a picture to explain. "Yeah. You know. You go into the store to buy something and have no idea where it is. You need help. A greeter comes up and says, 'May I help you?' What do people say?"

Without missing a beat, Nina answered, "No thanks, just looking."

Doug nodded. "Exactly. 'Just looking' is a conditioned response. We condition ourselves to avoid somebody trying to sell us things. We brush off that greeter with our conditioned response, even if we are wrong. We say we are just looking, but in reality, we need that help. It's a bad habit—that 'just looking' comeback. Once we learn any conditioned response, it's tough to control. We just respond without thinking. Seems like Retti did that to me. She was preoccupied and just said, 'No.'"

Nina looked up at her dad, her eyebrows raised, and asked, "Could you give it another try? Maybe?"

Doug thought for a minute and said, "Hmm. I've got an idea. Now don't get too excited, Nina. Once you ask somebody something and you get a firm 'no,' it's really hard to open their mind back up to change their position. But I'll try!"

Tips from the Communication Toolbox

- *Balance the effort you put in to solve any difficulty with the severity of the issue. Don't allow your mind to fester, causing you to complicate a minor problem and turn it into a major disaster.*
- *Take the time you need to make decisions—but avoid procrastination.*
- *List the positives and negatives when making tough decisions. Write them down. Creating a visual record offers you the opportunity to see the positives and negatives with a new perspective, helping you choose the most effective pathway.*
- *Anticipate what people might have as concerns. Don't let their doubts prevent you from implementing your successful persuasion plan. Preplan a pathway to overcome each and every one of those possible concerns.*
- *Relaxed people are more open to new thoughts and ideas than people consumed with personal issues.*
- *When asking for a major decision, break the concept down into small questions that build to that final big decision.*

CHAPTER 3

ACCEPTANCE

Concepts:

There are choices and decisions—opportunities with each. Your eyes must be open to them. Like the preacher who was warned, but refused to leave his church threatened by an imminent flood, don't ignore the signs. As water rose up the church steps, the preacher waved away the canoe his parishioners brought to save him. Instead, he prayed. He waved off the speed boat they offered as the water reached the height of the altar. As he stood on the roof, water about to crest over it, he waved off the helicopter the coast guard sent too. He drowned. Asking God why he had been forsaken, God said, "I sent you a canoe, a speed boat, and a helicopter. You were not forsaken—but you did fail to recognize and accept opportunity!" Let's dive into the methods to ensure you never miss an opportunity.

Doug Ross and Jason Bonner met years ago when both applied to join the fire department at Master Station on the same day. They got to know each other while they waited for their interviews. Jason had second thoughts about the lifestyle that goes with being a fireman. He was engaged to be married and on his way to a family life. Plus, he had the option of working at his family business, The Bonner Hotel. Doug had yet to propose to Loretta so the hours were no issue for him. Even though their time together that day was short, Doug and Jason kept in touch and developed a strong friendship that lasted.

The phone rang at The Bonner Hotel. The caller was Doug. "Hey Jason. It's me!"

"Douglas Ross! I was just thinking about you. Really was. Haven't seen you in weeks. We just completed the remodel of The Bonner Hotel breakfast room. How about popping by—want you to see it?"

"Great," Doug said. "You end breakfast at eleven so I'll get there by ten o'clock. I have something you might help me with. That work?"

Without hesitation Jason said, "Sure! Tell Millie I'm expecting you. You remember Millie, right? Our receptionist?"

Doug could picture her perfectly. He answered, "Of course. We've gotten to be friends. Grey hair, beautiful smile, soothing voice. Millie!"

"Yep. That's Millie. Hate to lose her. She's retiring, you know."

"I didn't. Thanks for telling me. I will wish her well. See you around ten."

Doug was known for his punctuality. If he said ten o'clock, you could bank on it. As the clock struck ten, Millie looked up from the reservations desk. The Reservations Manager was out so Millie had her hands full. She found herself dealing with momentary chaos. The phones kept ringing. People were impatiently standing in line. But Millie still had the forethought to give Doug one of her famous big smiles.

Doug joined the line with three impatient people ahead of him. The lady directly in front had some folded papers in her right hand. She kept slapping them into her left palm, obviously frustrated with waiting. The best way for Doug to help Millie was to break the silence. When people are engaged in conversation, time flies and impatience vanishes. But how could Doug break the silence? Doug was thinking, "*Hey lady. Stop slapping those papers. It's driving all of us crazy.*" But starting a war wouldn't help relax anybody.

From the back, the lady in front of Doug had brown hair—nothing special, a long dark jacket like so many other people wear, and jeans—nothing special at all. Nothing Doug could find to allow a sincere compliment. Then he saw her shoes. "Wow! Hot shoes! Shiny red—love 'em!" Doug said, loud enough for all to hear. Realizing the lady with the red shoes might get the wrong impression and think some guy was hitting on her, Doug quickly added, "My wife would love a pair like that. Where'd you get 'em?"

The lady turned, smiled and said, "These are recycled plastic. I love them. Just got 'em last week." She reached into her bag and handed Doug a coupon. "I got this coupon for twenty percent off if I place another order within thirty days. Too soon for me. You are welcome to it."

"Gosh, love it. You sure?" She nodded and Doug said, "Thank you so much. I truly appreciate it!"

"Delighted to help," she replied. But rather than ending there, she bought herself the potential of a future favor from Doug by saying, "I know you'd do the same for me, right?" Doug grinned and nodded.

When Doug's turn came, he was still feeling proud. He knew he had made a difference, whether others realized it or not. "Hi Millie. I'm here to see Jason. He's expecting me."

"There's a table in the breakfast room in the corner with a 'reserved' sign. That's for you. I'll tell Mr. Bonner you're here."

"Thanks Millie—and I want to say I have always felt sincerity from you when I've come here. You make people feel that you really care. I'll miss you. Any special plans?"

"I'll be here through the summer, but then I'm a free girl. A little travel. Watch some sunrises. Hang out with hubby. Spoil the grandkids. Stuff I never have time for now. And I have always enjoyed interacting with you, Mr. Ross. You never have made me feel like some of the patrons here do. You have always treated me with respect, and I thank you for that," Millie admitted.

Doug looked at Millie and could see tears beginning to glisten in Millie's eyes. To avoid any possibility of an embarrassing moment, as he turned and headed to the breakfast room he said, "I love you too—but enough of this mutual admiration event—gotta' get some breakfast with Jason. I'll catch you on my way out, okay?"

Jason Bonner had the distinction of being the great-grandson of Stuart Bonner, the man who founded Bonnerville. Though he could have become one of the privileged people who act like they own the world, Jason was a humble man who loved people. It was obvious. He was built like Santa Claus and had a laugh to match. If he grew a white beard along with his already flowing grey hair, he'd be the perfect St. Nick!

As Jason walked in, Doug stood up from their reserved table and reached out his hand. Jason, being the perpetual extrovert, pushed Doug's arm away and went in for a bear hug. As they slapped each other on the back, Jason loudly proclaimed to all, "Hey everybody. This is my good friend, Doug Ross. He was a team leader at Master Station Fire. I just found out—he's been promoted. Meet your new Fire Chief! Come on everybody—give it up for Doug!"

Dozens of people at breakfast applauded. Even the out-of-towners were clapping, though many didn't know why. But it did make Doug feel good. Jason was a master at celebrating his friends. The two sat down, and Doug enthusiastically said, "Let me congratulate you on this breakfast room—if that's what you call it. It looks more like a fine-dining restaurant. Beautiful!"

"Don't know if you remember the story, but when The Bonner was built by my grandad, we had breakfast, lunch, and dinner served here. Over the years he built up The Bonner to achieve a five-star hotel rating too. We were a five-star hotel, with a five-star restaurant. By the time I took over, things had changed. The more activities offered here in

Bonnerville, the busier our guests got. Now they fill their days off-site, so I closed out the lunch menu. Then I had to rethink dinner. I cut staff and realized we couldn't cover an unexpected rush. We were pissing people off. Since there are great places to eat not far from here, we killed dinner too. I should have thought through the ramifications before we stopped serving lunch. Now I use the staff when we are going to make changes. I get everybody's input. They always come up with things I miss. Gotta' trust the team."

Doug enthusiastically agreed. "At the firehouse, we live and die as a team—literally. All businesses are like that. Some managers just don't see it clearly enough."

"Well, I finally did!" Jason said. "With everybody's input, we decided to concentrate on breakfast. Really scrutinizing the numbers, we found we could not survive with just our own guests coming down for breakfast, so we had to make it special. People will travel to get here, as long as we make the experience worth the trip. We plowed serious cash into it. We brought it up to the standards we had when it was set up for fine dining—back to high polished wood floors, spacious tables, stuffed chairs, creative accent lighting, cloth napkins, and real silverware. We did it all!"

"You sure did! I really love your new open fireplace. It's massive! Love the aroma you get when oak logs grace the hearth."

"Don't go poetic on me now, Doug." Jason laughed. "But hey—look around. It works. But let's get back to you. You said you could use my help? What can I do for you, brother?"

"I wanted to pick your brain about Nina. You know everybody in town who's hiring, and she needs a job. Then you told me about Millie. You find a replacement for her?"

"Right," Jason said. "I remember—Nina graduated high school this year. We send her a gift card to celebrate. No college?"

"Well, she's still thinking about that. She and her buddy, Jaxie, want to take the summer and road trip the USA. I'm good with that, but Jaxie already has her college plan for the fall locked up. I told Nina she could go, but only for the summer, and if she doesn't apply to school before summer and have an acceptance letter in her hands before the fall session, she'd better have a job lined up."

Jason grinned. "I can read your mind. You're thinking Nina could replace Millie, aren't you? Did Millie tell you she's here all summer and will leave in September?"

"She did," Doug said. With a sheepish grin, Doug added, "You can read my mind. So, what do you think? You know Nina pretty well, right?"

Jason enthusiastically replied, "How funny. Nina Ross, my bud's little girl, working with us at The Bonner. I love the idea!"

"Great," Doug said.

On his drive home, Doug felt a sense of accomplishment. He got Nina that job! But something felt wrong. He couldn't put his finger on what it was. This nagging feeling of doubt wouldn't go away. As his anxiety began to overflow, he got an idea. He decided to get help, so he made a call.

Phil Stone's cell was on silent mode, but buzzed in his pocket. It was Douglas Ross in his caller ID. "Hey Doug! How you doin'?"

"Great, Phil, and you?"

Doug was irritated about something. Phil could hear it in his voice. Hoping to make Doug laugh, Phil said, "I was just sittin' here, wishin' and hopin'."

Still serious, Doug asked, "Wishing for what?"

With a smile in his voice, Phil said, "I was just sittin' here wishin' and hopin' you would call me!"

"Right!" Doug did laugh. "Guess you got your wish! I'm callin'!" With his genuine laugh, Doug relaxed—an example of the power of laughter. He said, "Just had the weirdest thing happen. You got a minute? Like to see if you have any insight. Bet you do!"

Phil chuckled, "My turn to be on the spot again, I guess. Okay. Whatcha' got?"

"I think I pulled off the deal of a lifetime, but something about it is bothering me." Doug paused, gathering his thoughts. "For Nina to go on a summer trip with her bud, Jaxie, I needed to help her find a job for this fall. You know how sometimes things seem to happen as if they were meant to be?"

"The longer I live, the more I see that. Makes me wonder if it's my guardian angel watchin' out," Phil said.

"I was feeling just like that. Nina needed a job. I found out Millie, the receptionist at The Bonner Hotel, is leaving after this summer. What incredible timing. My buddy, Jason Bonner, said he'd hire Nina. But he didn't seem totally on board with the idea. It's still gnawing at me."

Phil tried to picture the interaction, "You were at The Bonner with Jason and he said he'd hire Nina? Where's the problem?"

Doug said, "I don't know. I'm not sure. He had a strange look on his face, like he had a question he wanted to ask that he never got out."

Phil said, "Let me tell you a quick story. You just discovered the importance of watching peoples' eyes. The look in their eyes will give you powerful insight into their thoughts. I was managing a salesforce. Through the grapevine I heard rumors—one of my strongest and most tenured salespeople was interviewing with another company. My immediate objective was to convince him to stay. The blunt question in my mind was, *Are you quitting?* Far too direct. If he did plan to leave, with his answer he'd justify his thinking—he'd be selling me—and he'd be selling himself on leaving. Asking a point-blank question could force a decision I don't want.

"So, instead of directly confronting him, I asked what was on his mind, hoping he might open up without me having to ask a direct question. I couldn't let him get defensive. It didn't work. He said all was good. Nothing more.

"Still trying to stay with a non-confrontational question, I asked, 'I've heard a rumor you might be considering leaving us. Any truth to that?'

"Then he opened up. He admitted being torn between staying and going with the other company and their aggressive offer. I took the better part of an hour building doubt and uncertainty in his mind. What if he went with another company and it didn't work out? Then I painted the picture of a bright future for him if he stayed. No matter what I said, I couldn't get him off the fence. He just would not make a decision!

"I rummaged around and found a shiny quarter, and said, 'Let's flip a coin. Heads you stay, tails you leave?' He nodded."

Doug was astonished. "Wow!" he said. "That was risky, wasn't it? Unless you were cheating, you have no control over the coin. I know you better than that. You don't cheat. But what if it came up tails?"

Phil grinned and said, "Not risky at all. I had a plan. I remembered when that coin flip idea first came to me. It was when we went to Disney World with my three-year-old little boy, Bryan, many years ago. I learned a new perspective about the importance of visual clues to what someone is thinking.

"We took Bryan to Disney World. We all loved it. But then the problem. He couldn't decide between the Pirates of the Caribbean pistol or the sword as his souvenir. Disney won't let you exit rides without going through a souvenir shop. I had to get Bryan something. It didn't matter to me which he picked. I just wanted him to make a choice so we could get moving. He could not choose. As he waffled back and forth, I came up with an idea.

"I pulled a quarter out of my pocket and said, 'Let's let the coin decide. Heads and you get the sword—tails and you get the pistol. Okay?' I squatted down so he was at eye level, flipped the quarter and caught it. Then I asked, 'You ready?' He nodded again. I lifted the hand covering the coin, but I didn't look at it—I only watched Bryan. I was looking for any sign of emotion when the coin revealed his prize. There sure was emotion! He was disappointed! The coin showed heads. Heads meant the sword, but the expression on Bryan's face told me he wanted the pistol. I asked, 'You're a little disappointed, aren't you? I can see it in your eyes. You really want the pistol?' Bryan nodded again and gave me a cute impish grin, and we bought him the pistol.

"I decided to use that strategy with my wobbling sales guy. I was confident with either outcome when I flipped that coin. Heads and he would stay—just what I wanted. If it came up tails, I expected to see regret in his eyes—obvious disappointment. I planned to say, 'You really want to stay, don't you?' I was ready either way, heads or tails.

"The coin bounced on my desk and finally settled. It was heads. My sales guy looked at it and said, 'Well that was easy.' I got a strong handshake…and he stayed with me and the company!"

Doug shook his head. "You must have a story for everything, don't you?"

Phil nodded. "I try to. Stories open people to new perspectives—new ways to see things. When I want to change people's minds, a relevant story is a top priority for me."

"I can see that," Doug said. "Any thoughts on Jason and that look in his eyes?"

"Tell him!" Phil said. "Stop back at The Bonner and tell him something was bothering you. Just be yourself, and be honest. Tell him you saw something in his eyes that told you he wasn't totally settled with Nina. Don't just ignore it. Jason may be concerned about something. It could fester if you don't deal with it."

"Yep. I do need to deal with it," Doug agreed.

"And look at you. You are already struggling with it. I can hear stress in your voice."

Doug said, "Lots of people read between the lines. Phil, you listen between the lines." Doug paused, as he thought about Jason. "Hey. You know what? I'm turning the car around and going back. It's bothering me, and probably bothering Jason too. Need to solve it!"

"Perfect!" Phil said.

Minutes later Doug was knocking on Jason Bonner's office door. "Hey Doug. You're back! You forget something?"

"Kinda'. On my way home I couldn't stop thinking about a strange look you had when you agreed to hire Nina. You had some issues. I could tell. I could see it in your eyes. You had a question in your eyes. I should have brought it up then."

Jason laughed. "In my eyes! Right. You saw a question in my eyes. Bet I know. It's your sales buddy you told me about, Phil, right? Something he taught so you can sell people?"

Doug shook his head, "Yeah—Phil. But it's not about selling people. It's about helping people. Phil told me not to make a mistake so many people do. People pay such close attention to the words they pick, and what to say, they forget to pay attention to the other person. They don't see all the visual input. There is so much to learn, but you gotta' do both—watch and listen—closely! Seriously, I could see concern in your eyes. So, rather than ignore it, I came back here to help figure it out with you. I can help you if I know what you are thinking. Make sense?"

"Okay, it does. So what was that 'question in my eyes' thing? How's that work?"

Doug explained. "Phil told me a story—a story about reading people's minds. Let me give you the punch-line. This story was when Phil almost lost one of his top sales guys and convinced him to stay—with a quarter."

Puzzled, Jason asked, "A quarter—like a coin—a quarter?"

"Yep. Phil had a salesperson about to quit, but hadn't totally made up his mind. Phil convinced the guy a coin flip could help make the decision."

Jason shook his head. "That doesn't sound smart. What if the coin came up wrong?"

"Phil had both sides covered. If the coin came up heads, the guy would stay. If it came up tails, Phil expected to see signs of disappointment in the sales guy's eyes. Either way, Phil was ready with a pathway to keep his sales guy from quitting."

"That's different," Jason said. "Never heard anything like that before, but I can see how to use it. Any time there are two choices—neither the obvious choice, flip a coin and watch their eyes for any emotional reaction. You see emotion, you can tell what they are thinking. I like it."

"So," Doug said. "About Nina working with the team here at The Bonner—what's your question?"

"Well, to be honest with you…," Jason paused to find the right words.

Doug jumped in. "Aha. You see? When I asked about Nina, I could tell something was bothering you. Now, when you tell me what you were thinking, I can help you solve it. I'm helping you!"

Jason grinned as he explained, "Well—I need to replace Millie, but I have time. She's not leaving until the end of summer. That works. And there is not a ton of training needed for the job. Nina just has to learn customer service. We know how to teach that. Plus, Nina has a smooth, soothing voice and a great smile—both keys to help relax people. It's just that I don't want Nina to work here for a couple months and then I have to find a replacement for her too. That's all."

Doug looked at Jason and raised his eyebrows as he asked, "If Nina could give you at least a year, would that work? Could you make that work?" Doug prodded, trying not to sound too needy.

"I like Nina," Jason said. "I know she'd do great here, and she's coachable. Tell you what—if I can get at least a year, and if she'll agree to train her replacement before she leaves, let's do it. Have her call and I'll go through the requisite interview, but, between you and me—she's got it. I have no doubts, no concerns. Really. Let's do it!"

That following Saturday afternoon, only three days remained before Jaxie was to pick up the RV. Doug was dealing with a time crunch, and a task he was dreading—changing Loretta's mind. But he had armed himself with a powerful plan.

Doug and Loretta were done for the day, sitting on the family room couch together, TV on in the background. As he swirled his wine glass and lifted it up to toast, he proclaimed, "This is to us getting through a tough week!"

Their glasses clinked, and Retti let out a soft sigh. Doug watched as she slipped off her shoes, putting her feet on a pillow on their coffee table. He could see the stress of the week fading from Retti's face. He decided it was time to see if he could change her mind about Nina's proposed road trip.

"I'm so proud of you, babe," Doug said. He knew a compliment would be a great start. If she sensed the compliment was fake, she'd smell a rat right away. Doug was fully aware his praise had to be genuine and sincere. But it was always easy for Doug to gush about Retti. They were a 'happily ever after' couple. "Your practice is a screaming success. Seems like everybody loves you. And I'm getting the hang of the Chief position at the firehouse. We're doing great. Even Nina. She graduated close to the top of her class. So proud of her too. Have you talked with her about college?"

Retti reached over and squeezed Doug's hand and said, "I love you too!" She took a breath—then continued. "Nina? I don't know. She told me lots of her friends are terrified of debt, and the monstrous cost of a major college degree. They're going right into the workforce."

"Really? Ya' think that's what Nina plans?" Doug asked, not letting the conversation seem too serious.

"Not sure. I get the point, though. I'm not going to be one of those 'helicopter parents' and micro-manage her life. She's a smart girl. She'll find her path. We're just here to support her, agree?"

Doug took a sip of wine and said, "Yeah. Give her some space. I agree." He looked down, swishing the wine in his glass, and looked up at Retti. "I stopped in to see Jason the other day. I was in the area and he just redid the breakfast dining area at The Bonner."

"I've always liked Jason Bonner. How's he doing?"

"Real well. Hotel is kicking butt and lookin' beautiful—better than ever," Doug responded. Then he asked, "You remember Jason's receptionist, Millie?"

"Sure. What a great hire she was. The first person a customer interacts with is just like when you sit down to watch a new movie. If the film doesn't grab you in the first few minutes, it's missed the mark. First impressions are critical. Millie does an awesome job making people who are checking in at The Bonner feel like she's a friend of theirs. Her warmth is so addicting. People instantly like her."

"Jason is gonna' need somebody special to replace her," Doug casually said.

"Millie's leaving? Oh, too bad."

"Jason is a great boss. Over breakfast I mentioned that he'd be somebody I'd trust to manage our Nina," Doug added. Retti just nodded, sipping her wine. "Yeah. I told him Nina would be looking for a job if she didn't land a college acceptance soon. Too bad Millie isn't leaving until September."

"Why is that too bad? Jason has her for summer," Retti asked, not sounding like she cared about the answer.

"Because he told me he'd love it if Nina could be his new receptionist. He thinks the world of her, ya' know. But I told Jason I didn't know if it could work because you and I want her to either do college or get a job."

"We did. I put my foot down," Retti said. "But I do like the idea of Nina at The Bonner. It would be a great start for Nina. It was job or college. This would be a great job for Nina. And I do like Jason. What do you think, babe?"

Doug set his glass down and asked, "Should I tell him Nina could start in September? Nina could take the summer and chill. It could be an extra graduation gift—a reward for the great grades." Doug watched Retti's facial expression. She still seemed calm and relaxed. Sounding as if the idea had just popped into his head, Doug said, "Boy. Imagine how blown away Nina would be if we told her she had the job at The Bonner, and since she can't start until fall, we were going to let her go with Jaxie on that road trip she had her heart set on."

Retti sat there, calmly taking it in. There was no sign of negativity—no sign that when Doug would finally ask the big question, there would be anything but a positive response. She seemed to agree with everything so far. Doug took a deep breath and confidently asked, "What do ya' think, babe? Bonner and road trip for our graduate? I'd like to help her make that happen." Then Doug added a smooth alternate of choice question. "You pick. You can tell her if you want, or I can. You want to tell her?"

Retti stood up and started to laugh. "You sly dog, you. I get it. The wine. The compliments. How wonderful Jason is. Millie. All that—you set me up! You sat there selling me, didn't you? From what you've told me about him, I bet your buddy, Phil, helped you come up with this."

"Not Phil on this one. It was Jaxie and Nina. Last Saturday they sat on this very couch and asked me little questions. They got me thinking. It was like they took me by the hand and gently walked me through their plan. Step by step they helped me see a different perspective, avoiding any question I could answer with, 'No!' I was gradually being sold. It actually felt good. I got excited."

Retti shook her head. "The girls? How 'bout that? Well, you did a good job too. I've grown to love the idea. You kinda' laid it out slowly, piece by piece. My mindset gradually transitioned from being a total 'no' on the road trip to accepting the idea she would start working after summer, and she could have the summer off. Why not? I do…I love it. For doing such a great job, you get to tell Nina!"

Summer passed like summers do. Blink and it's over. But, as promised, Doug and Retti got their selfie pic the girls took when they checked into each RV park and settled in for the night. Doug was saving them all. Preserving life's precious times through documenting was a special joy for Doug. He planned to make a collage of the trip to give to each of the girls. Their 'trip of a lifetime' would be vividly remembered.

Tips from the Communication Toolbox

- *Watch for opportunity. Answer the door when opportunity knocks. Keep your eyes and ears open. Don't wear noise-canceling headphones when you should be paying attention.*
- *When someone thanks you, don't say, "No problem," and end there. Secure a future favor by adding, "You'd do the same for me, right?"*
- *Never miss an opportunity to publicly celebrate your friends.*
- *Make decisions with your team, rather than going it alone.*
- *A mind-reader pays attention to both verbal and non-verbal signals.*

- *Compliments must be genuine.*
- *Win their trust with a powerful first impression.*
- *Big ideas are easily swallowed one small bite at a time.*

CHAPTER 4

EVALUATION

> Concepts:
>
> Let's look at how to lead people, so when they answer your question, it's the answer you want. Tap into their thoughts. Learn what appeals to them. Carefully evaluate the situation. Avoid conflict, allow misgivings, and don't confront people with their mistakes. Keep your eyes open. Recognize the possible negative outcomes—and prevent them! Here's how:

"Welcome to The Bonner, Nina. I've been so looking forward to this. You met Millie when I brought you in for an interview," Jason Bonner said.

"I met Millie. Liked her."

"Perfect. I'm going to have you shadow her for your first week. Then, if you are comfortable, I'll have you take the lead."

"Great Mr. Bonner," Nina replied, nodding.

"I love how attentive you are. Most folks, younger than I, aren't great at eye contact. Bet your dad worked with you on that." Nina smiled and nodded, even more aggressively. "Let me tell you a little story, how I began to figure out what makes people tick."

"Great," Nina said as she watched Jason sit back in his chair and gently put his feet on the blotter on his desk. Nina could tell this was not to be a short story.

He began, "My dad accepted a new job when I was just out of grade school. That meant we would move from Bonnerville to a house about an hour west, not far from the Box River. Since I knew no one, I spent that summer exploring Babian Forest Preserve and the Box River valley.

"Every day families would drive for hours to Babian Forest Preserve to picnic and fish. These folks would sit in the shadow of the old windmill that landmarked Babian and fish all day long. Most folks never even got a fish to bite, no matter what they tried for bait. Nina, fish won't bite if the bait has no appeal to them. It was a great lesson for me. I realized people won't bite if the bait has no appeal. Get what I mean?"

"I guess," Nina replied, not sounding convinced. "You can't hook a fish without the right bait, and the same goes with people?" she asked.

Jason smiled. "Almost. But we are not trying to hook people. We are trying to help them. The choices we offer must interest them—or we fail. Some folks vacation in Bonnerville to hike and do some basic mountain climbing. But, if our guests have zero interest in mountain climbing, no point in trying to interest them in mountain climbing equipment." Jason paused. "Think of it this way: What you offer must have appeal. At The Bonner we find out if sightseeing appeals to guests. If it doesn't, we don't offer sightseeing options. But if they are excited about sightseeing, if they show interest, we can offer sightseeing possibilities our guests will be inclined to appreciate."

"I get you now," Nina said, nodding. "I need to investigate someone's interest level before offering options. If there is no interest, I can try to create interest. But if there still is no interest, I need to go in another direction. I need different 'bait.' Interesting perspective, Mr. Bonner."

He laughed. "Yeah. The lessons of a fisherman. And there's more. I decided to teach those failed fishermen the fine art of fishing on the Box River. Years earlier Grandpa taught me the more hooks you have in the water, the more likely you are to catch fish. It was a great lesson, not only for the world of fishing, but for countless other aspects of everyday life. I grabbed the cornflakes box from the pantry, three fishing poles and a stringer, and headed off to the river."

Nina was confused. "Cornflakes? Why cornflakes? Cornflakes a favorite of yours?" she asked.

Jason shook his head. "Used to love 'em, until I made them into dough balls to catch fish. That killed my passion for eating them. You won't find cornflakes on the menu at The Bonner." Jason smiled and winked at Nina, then continued. "And I didn't want my secret of cornflakes to get out so I put the box in a brown paper bag. As usual, people were fishing all over Babian Forest Preserve. I went way downriver until I came upon a secluded cove. No one was there—only me. The sun lit the trees above. The summer air refreshed. The river current was soft and gentle in that cove. What could be more perfect? It was time for catching!

"I set my poles down, grabbed the cornflakes, dumped a pile in my hands, stuck them in the water and started squeezing. As my golf ball sized cornflake ball sat drying in the sun, I squeezed off a pinch and molded it around my fishhook. Then I cast it in the water about twenty feet out.

"I set the pole on the ground and cradled the pole tip in a 'Y' shaped stick. Before I could get the second pole ready, it happened.

Bam! The line went taught. The pole bounced violently. I lunged for it and grabbed the handle just as it was about to disappear in the river. I thought, '*Woah! This must be a big one!*' It was. This went on non-stop. I had half-a-dozen fish in less than a half-hour."

Nina had always liked fishing. Her dad used to take her to the Box River when she was little. Spending the day alone with her dad, picnicking on the river's edge, made her feel so special. The memories always brought a smile to her face and joy to her heart. She was loving this fish story. "And you never even used that third pole?" she asked.

Jason, eyebrows raised, asked, "Better to have more poles than you need, or need more poles than you have?" He looked at Nina. Her eyebrows were raised too. She was nodding her head. He knew she understood, so Jason continued. "I decided to carry the fish all the way home to prove my fish story. The shortest way home was back through Babian.

"As I walked, I realized people all over Babian were staring and pointing—at me. One lady playfully slapped the guy with her. 'Look at that boy. He's got fish. You got nothing!' Made me smile.

"One guy, sitting in a folding chair holding his fishing pole, dropped it and ran up to me. 'You catch those?' he asked.

"As I kept walking, I just said, 'Yep.'"

"Whatcha' gonna' do with 'em? You gonna' eat 'em?" he asked, as he tried to catch up with me.

"Rather than tell him my plan was to show Mom and then bury the fish under our trees for fertilizer, I said, 'Not sure. Why do you ask?' If I had just told him I was going to use these fish to fertilize our trees, none of this story would have happened. It made me realize the importance of understanding what people were thinking before I blurted out some answer. Knowing their thoughts often highlighted opportunities for me.

"The guy responded to my question saying, 'Well, if you are gonna' eat 'em…that's a lot of fish. Maybe you could sell me one or two? How 'bout a quarter apiece?'

"There was a Dairy Queen on my way home, and carrying an ice cream cone rather than some smelly fish was an easy choice. I dangled those fish in front of him. With an excited grin on my face I said, 'And you can tell everybody it was you who caught them!'

"His face lit up with a huge smile. I gave him all six fish, took the money, and stifled a victory scream as I walked up the hill toward Dairy Queen. Every day, weather permitting, I headed for the Box River. And every day I cashed in. I loved it. I even dreamed about becoming a professional fisherman—you know—the sportsmen you see making their living with sports videos and endorsements."

Nina enthusiastically said, "Wish I had been there. I would have loved it too. But I'm glad you didn't become a sports fisherman." She sat quietly. She could feel Mr. Bonner's curiosity as she said, "If you were a pro sports fisherman…you wouldn't be here! Neither would I!"

Jason just shook his head and grinned. Sitting up straight in his chair, he changed the tone. "I'm all about The Bonner now. So, let's get back to that, okay?" Nina nodded. "Nobody's perfect. We all know that. But at The Bonner, we need to strive for perfection."

Jason watched as Nina opened her notepad, and he continued. "When I was in school, my parents expected good grades. Straight 'A's' is what my folks demanded. I was expected to do excellent work. No 'B, C, or D' allowed. Thank God I never got an 'F.' They might have kicked me out of the house!" Jason laughed. So did Nina. "I learned I did not have to be anywhere near perfect. In some classes, I could take a test and get a bunch wrong and still get that 'A.' My schooling was always consistent. Never was I required to be perfect. Education should prepare us for the real world, right? Does it?" Jason paused. Nina could tell his question was rhetorical, so she sat quietly, keeping her eyes glued on Jason.

"Many professions require one hundred percent efficiency. A mistake may happen, but it must be a rare event. Think of the guy who does your income taxes. Nice if he got it perfect. Picture your brain surgeon. Ninety percent by that guy won't get an 'A.'

"I've always wondered about the folks who forecast the weather," Jason said.

Puzzled, Nina said, "Huh? What do you wonder about?"

"I remembered an old weatherman buddy of mine. I tried kidding him about weather reports. I said, 'I'd bet no one is holding your feet to the fire when you miss a forecast. And you guys all use that percent chance stuff. There's a fifty percent chance of rain. If it rains, you were right. If it doesn't, you were right.' He was incensed. I could not believe his reaction. He went on and on explaining how weather predicting is constantly improving. He pulled up statistics that proved their ever-increasing accuracy and said technology plays a major role in their progress. He told me they have, and always will strive for one hundred percent accuracy—the key word here is 'strive.'

"Seriously, Nina. Here at The Bonner, no one grades you. But you will have tasks that need perfect execution for us to grow and thrive. Here, you don't get an 'A' for ninety or ninety-five percent like you did in school. Here we strive for perfect. If you aim for perfect and miss a tiny bit—not so bad. You get in the habit of settling for mediocre, and you miss a tiny bit—the team is in trouble. Make sense?"

"Interesting way to say that. I get it," Nina said. "I promise I'll go beyond knowing what to do just fairly well…"

Jason laughed. "I have to give you this—you do pay attention!"

"Yep. And I'll know what to do…or I'll ask for help. How's that? What you're looking for?"

With a huge smile on his face, Jason motioned for Nina to stand and follow him. "I'm good—real good. You are going to be great here. Let's get you to Millie."

The first week flew by. The following Monday found Nina behind the reservations counter sitting with Millie. Millie began, "Ya' know, Nina. You're catching on fast. Love it. When I first started, Mr. Bonner told me about his 'Silver Rule.' Ready?"

It was quiet time at The Bonner, after the breakfast rush and before check-out. With no interruptions, Millie explained. "Let's talk about our guests. People have so many rights, some God-given, some created by man, and one that should always be considered is one's right to make a mistake and atone, apologize, and move on. You know the golden rule—do unto others as you would have others do unto you?"

"Sure!" Nina answered. "I try my best to live by it."

"Mr. Bonner told me this when I first started and I've never forgotten. He called it his Silver Rule. Pretty simple. All people have the right to be wrong. That's how I remember to give space when someone tells me something I believe is wrong. The worst thing to do is challenge people. A challenge grows into a confrontation—conflict! Almost impossible to unravel a mess like that. Better to prevent it."

Nina said, "I can think of a ton of examples. Even road rage. One driver challenges another. They get pissed off and the next thing you know, one of those drivers does something stupid, all because of being challenged."

"You've got it. You will deal with customers who anger you. They will say things that make no sense. They will shout at the top of their lungs, and be dead wrong. It happens. If they make you mad, don't slap them back. It is not about you. It is about our customer. Don't make them pay by shaking your accusing finger in their face. Wrap your arms around them instead. Ask the right questions. Show them you are on their side. Always avoid challenging them."

Just then Jason Bonner walked up to the front desk and said, "I could hear you guys talking about my Silver Rule. Made me smile. Got a short little story that will help you remember, okay? Millie knows this one."

Millie looked at Nina and whispered, "You're gonna' love this."

Jason began, "Retailers in the early 1900's coined the phrase, 'The Customer is always right,' to ensure their employees would provide superlative customer service. Many business owners challenged this concept. They argued that customers can be dishonest and use this position of always being right to defraud the retailers. We don't even think about that here at The Bonner. When you deal with our guests, think of it this way: The guest is always right, but not always correct. Don't make them pay for their error."

"In other words," Nina jumped in, "Be patient with people—even when they are wrong."

"Exactly," said Jason. "And you can use this approach in every area of your life. When you are wronged, don't retaliate. Don't feel like you must get even. Remember the Silver Rule. Everyone has the right to be wrong. There's enough craziness out there. No point in creating more conflict."

"Makes sense," Nina said. "I even get bent out of shape when I do something, and I know it wasn't my best effort. I beat myself up enough. Hate when somebody else rubs it in."

"Give others the space to be wrong before judging them," Jason added. "Don't let yourself take a position where you expose them as being wrong. As you just said, Nina, don't rub in their error. When someone takes a position that is wrong, they may feel they are losing face if they admit their error. Find a way to tactfully let them off the hook."

Nina raised her eyebrows, nodded her head and grinned at Millie, telling her without words, she did love Jason's story.

Millie grinned back and said, "After lunch we'll talk about cancellations."

Returning from lunch, they were both energized and ready for more training. Millie began, "One great thing about The Bonner...we get few cancellations on our reservations. The national average right now is twenty-four percent. We hover around twenty percent. Mr. Bonner would like to see that number drop even further. We will go over that. We're also going to talk about Bonner's Law. He calls it that so we all remember it. It's just being aware of an impending negative and stopping it before it starts, so let's start there, with Bonner's Law, okay?"

"Bonner's Law? Can't wait! I've got my pad ready, Millie. Fire away," Nina said.

"Some cancellations are actually okay. School gets canceled on a snow day, or the school teacher cancels the final exam and gives everybody an 'A!' But most cancellations come with a loss, not a gain."

Nina jotted some notes as Millie broke down the cancellation issues. "If our guest cancels their reservation, it can be devastating. Sometimes we can rebook a room, and sometimes it goes empty. No revenue. No housekeeping. No breakfasts. Nothing. And once a guest cancels, it is close to impossible to change their minds and turn it around. The best way to turn around a cancellation is to prevent it in the first place. Not just in the hotel industry, but in every business. Any business dealing with cancellations should clearly understand this: Eliminate potential reasons people might cancel by asking pertinent questions. Stay positive, but don't ignore the potential negatives. You must always be looking for and evaluating what could go wrong. You ever hear about Murphy's Law?"

"Sure," Nina said. "Like—what could go wrong, does?"

"Yep. Here's a cute story for you," Millie said. "True story. Sometime in the late 1940's, an Air Force Captain named Edward Murphy was ordered to have his team set up gauges at Andrews Air Force base in California to help determine the amount of force the human body could handle in flight. Chuck Yeager broke the sound barrier and survived. How much more force could the human body endure? The Air Force needed to know. Captain Murphy would use those new gauges to figure it out.

"Sure enough, the gauges malfunctioned. Murphy, cursing through his failure, was credited for saying, 'If there is any way things can go wrong, they will!' The media interviewed the flight surgeon who had volunteered to be a guinea pig on these tests. The surgeon was quoted as saying, 'The team operated under Murphy's Law—what could go wrong, would!' The name 'Murphy's Law' became synonymous with the inevitability of a negative outcome with any endeavor. It has even become a reason people grasp to explain their failures. People say, 'We were victims of Murphy's Law.' It's even become a go-to excuse for people when they lose.

"Lots of things really do live under Murphy's Law. Those gauges could fail, and they did. The baby could wake and cry, and it does. The rockets could explode on the launch pad, and they do. The water could boil over. On and on. Murphy's Law: What could go wrong, does go wrong," Millie paused, and then added, "But not always!

"Ready?" Millie asked, her eyes darting about, surveying the room as if she was about to reveal something top secret and was afraid of an eavesdropper. She grinned as she said, "Here is Bonner's Law: What could go wrong, MIGHT go wrong!"

Nina reacted with a wince—like she had just heard something totally absurd. "What do you mean?" she asked.

Eyebrows up, Millie explained. "There is a glass filled to the brim with milk, and the child tries to carry it to the TV room. What could go wrong? The milk could spill. It is not inevitable. It is preventable. That's the essence of Bonner's Law. It might happen, but if we recognize the negative potential and take the appropriate action, we could prevent what could go wrong from actually going wrong.

"A cancellation means something went wrong. It happens in all types of businesses. Unlike many businesses, most of the time it has absolutely nothing to do with any mistake we made here at The Bonner. It's not them regretting what they bought, fearing they messed up. Usually the guest has some issue come up," Millie said.

"I get it. I've bought something and had buyer's remorse, regretting my purchase. Then I canceled it. Long time back, my dad ordered a custom fishing pole. When he saw their terrible reviews—he canceled it. I bet some guests make up stories to get out of a booking, right?" Nina asked.

"Good point. That's why Mr. Bonner initiated that twenty-four-hour cancellation clause every guest signs when they book with us. When people know they have to pay to cancel, and they cancel anyway, it's for a good reason. Mr. Bonner always likes to give people the benefit of the doubt. He waives that cancellation fee all the time. He says he'd want to be given some space if he were the guest, so they get space when they deal with Mr. Bonner—and all of us on the team. Another little 'golden rule' approach, right? Do unto others…"

Nina jumped in. "…Before they do unto you!" she said, as she started to laugh. Millie was grinning as Nina went on. "No, I know. Just trying to be funny."

Millie gave Nina one of her famous smiles. "It's been phrased a lot of ways, but it means to always be fair. But the place to dig deeper for the solution to cancellations is not when they call to cancel. It's when they make the reservation. Remember Bonner's Law. Prevent what could go wrong from actually going wrong.

"We went over those questions listed on that laminated sheet last week. You're good on why we use them and what they are for?" Millie asked.

"I think I've got it," Nina affirmed. "Those questions remind me of things I could ask when guests book their stay with us. I can also use them when guests check in. Those questions were designed to help us make our guests more comfortable."

"And they are," Millie agreed. "But more than that, those questions were crafted to find out about our guest's trip. By asking questions about their plan, we can take notes about all the things they are hoping to do. If it's business, what's their goal? Not business but sightseeing? What types of things do they want to see? We find these things out, take notes, and we can sell them on how The Bonner will satisfy all those wants and needs. We want them to get off the phone when they make that reservation really excited about their stay at The Bonner. That way, if something comes up, something minor, they may just deal with the issue so they can have that trip they have been totally sold on. It's not just cancellations here at The Bonner. It's for every day of your life. Think of Bonner's Law. Figure out what might go wrong and prevent it. Make sense?"

"One hundred percent, Millie! How about this?" Nina said, as she began to smile. "I'll ask those questions, the ones that fit, and I'll put their answers in our Customer Relationship Management system so the staff will have access to those answers too. That way, the entire team can support the desires of our guests."

"Perfect!" Millie announced. "No. More than perfect! That is a fabulous idea! We need to get with Mr. Bonner and outline this plan. He'll love it I'd bet." Millie glanced up and saw Mr. Bonner. Nina and Millie stood up as Millie said, "Mr. Bonner. Excuse us, but if you have a minute, Nina has come up with an idea."

He turned and went over to the reservations counter and said, "Love to hear it. Whatcha' got?"

Nina first thanked Millie for her support of the plan. Then she outlined it, thrilled to see Jason's face light up with approval. Nina stood tall behind the counter, basking in the glow of praise and recognition. "I want to thank you, Mr. Bonner. I never thought working would be fun. At The Bonner, it is. It's an amazing team. And you don't march around here barking orders. You truly listen. And you don't treat us like we're inferior—not on your level. I can feel the respect you give every one of us here."

"You are very welcome, Nina. The way I see it, I work for all you guys. You don't work for me. You work for the team, and for The Bonner. We support each other, and together we bury the negatives. The result? It's fun. It's just what they call servant leadership." Jason reached over the counter to shake Nina's hand and said, "Maybe you'll keep having so much fun here I can convince you to stay with us at The Bonner. Hope so."

Tips from the Communication Toolbox

- *If what you are selling has no appeal, stop trying to sell it. Go in another direction.*
- *With more hooks in the water, you catch more fish.*
- *When it comes to resources, have more than you need. Don't need more than you have.*
- *As you learn what people are thinking, you will find opportunities.*
- *Though unachievable, strive for perfection.*

- *Don't beat up someone for being wrong. All of us are wrong sometimes.*
- *Recognize possible negatives and eliminate them before they manifest themselves.*

CHAPTER 5

GO STEP-BY-STEP

Concepts:

You start a journey by putting the end destination into your GPS. It lays out the route, and all the course changes needed to get to the address. If you follow the directions—with an accurate GPS—you will go step by step, and reach your destination. Move someone to your way of thinking the same way the GPS moves you: step by step. You know where you want the conversation to go. That's your destination. Go there step by step. But with people, don't start with the destination like you do with your GPS. That would be like telling a joke, but starting with the punchline. Not the way to get a laugh! Watch Nina break down the complicated step-by-step.

Although her time with Millie was over, Nina felt inspired at The Bonner. She had fun interacting with the guests...most of the time. But things didn't stay all peaches and cream for Nina. Helping people, Jason's coaching, and her growing confidence sure had a positive impact. But complaints from the guests when something did go wrong were starting to eat away at her attitude.

As she was leaving for the day, one guest came up to the desk, and he screamed in Nina's face. His words were laced with profanity. Nina couldn't take the abuse. Tears rolled down her cheeks as she grabbed her phone and called the Maintenance Department. Nina was able to reassure the man that his issue would be handled, so by the time Maintenance got to the reception desk, he had calmed down.

Nina left the Bonner that day with her thoughts in turmoil. As she pulled the door closed on her Mustang, she couldn't ignore the pounding of her heart. Nina hated the tension that seemed to completely consume her when a guest exploded with complaints. These tirades occurred far too often. As much as Nina enjoyed the many positives she found at The Bonner, she dreaded the next guest blow-up. She had committed to stay at The Bonner for at least a year, but didn't see how in the world she could survive a full year of this abuse. As she stewed, out of nowhere a sudden feeling of hope swept over Nina. She remembered her dad telling her, "My buddy, Phil Stone, is a lifelong salesperson. He's a strong communicator. Now you are at The Bonner, if you ever need help with what to say and how to say it, try Phil. He loves to coach people."

Nina thought, *"I'll call Phil Stone!"*

Phil's caller ID showed it was Nina calling. "Hey Nina. How are you...and how may I help you?"

"Mr. Stone, thanks for taking my call. I'm well, and you?"

"I'm good—and please—call me Phil. Your dad and I have gotten to be pretty good friends, ya' know. You don't need to be so formal with the 'Mister,' though I do appreciate the respect it shows when a younger person talks with an older guy like me."

"Aw. You're young," Nina said, as she moved past the potentially uncomfortable topic of age. "My dad says you are a polished salesperson. I don't know why Dad suggested I call you, but he did," Nina said, her uncertainty painfully obvious. She and Phil had only met a handful of times and just chatted about nothing, so they didn't know each other very well. Phil wanted to be tactful so she would be comfortable giving him more details. He had to find simple, non-threatening questions to learn what Nina was thinking.

"So, you were talking with your dad about something and he said you should call me? What were you guys talking about?"

"The Bonner Hotel."

Phil wanted to know more so simply replied, "Bonner Hotel?"

"Yeah. They just hired me as their receptionist. It was part of a deal I made with Dad to go on a trip," she replied.

Again he chose a short question to get more details before he tried to help. He needed to understand fully, so only said, "Oh?"

That opened Nina's floodgates. "I started at The Bonner a while ago. I like the people there. Millie, their old receptionist, trained me, and the job isn't hard. It's just some easy data work and I answer the phones, but almost everybody who calls or comes down after check-in is pissed off about something." Nina was shaking her head. "No, it's not everybody, but it sure feels like it some days. I don't know what to do. It makes me crazy. Millie made a joke of it. She laughed as she told me, 'It's always like this—we've been pissing people off for years, I guess.' I thought she was kidding. Boy was I wrong." Nina's tone stayed so serious. "She tells me I'll get used to it. I wake up in the morning and dread going in 'cause I know it's gonna' be people yelling at me again. I can't quit. I need to figure this out. Dad said you might help, even though I don't sell products."

"Don't know if I can, but I sure would be honored to try. How 'bout I buy you a smoothie? We can chat over lunch tomorrow. That work?"

"Tomorrow for lunch? Okay, great!" The apprehension in Nina's voice was gone, replaced by genuine enthusiasm. "I'm looking forward to it. Where should we go?"

"I'll meet you at Soothie-Smoothie at noon. I see that black Mustang of yours parked there all the time."

Bonnerville was a medium size city with a small-town feel. At six stories, The Bonner Hotel was one of the biggest buildings in town. Only the Allworld Insurance Company building at the town center was taller. The snowcapped mountains in the distance made this heartland city a perfect vacation destination. Soothie-Smoothie was just down the road from Allworld and only a couple blocks from Bonnerville High School. When school let out, Soothie-Smoothie was packed with kids. But with school in session, lunchtime was quiet and a perfect place to talk. Once they got settled, Nina opened up.

"Just yesterday I had a woman named Jill who was steaming mad. She came down to our front desk, ready for battle. Before I could even get a word out, she went on a rant. Her hotel room shower would not stop running. She told me she picked up her room phone to get help. Our menu is printed on the phone. She figured the most likely source of support was Guest Services. She pushed the button for that extension. Instead of getting help, she found herself listening to our music on hold. She said a voice finally broke through. She tried to ask a question, but got no response, and suddenly realized that voice was automated. She said, 'It was phone tree hell!' I hate to admit it, but I could feel her pain. I've been there myself in a hotel trying to get help. Not with a wicked phone tree, but with a damned soda machine."

Phil sat there slowly stirring his smoothie with his double-wide straw as he concentrated on Nina. She needed to get her frustration out, so he let her vent.

"Mr. Stone…uh…Phil. Jaxie and I were wrapping up our summer trip. Our last night was awful. I was on my cell grouping the gazillions of pictures I took of our trip when Jaxie hit the brakes and let out this horrified scream. She yelled, 'What?'"

"I looked up as she turned into the Crescent Motel parking lot. 'Grab me my notebook,' Jaxie directed. 'Look at this picture! Now look at this place!' Jaxie was fuming. The brochure pictured a beautiful two-story building with a balcony off of every room. The building was shaped like a crescent. The shot from the room was a breathtaking view of the valley below with snowcapped mountains in the distance. Instead, in front of us was a typical two-story motel with the first-floor rooms all opening right into the parking lot, and the second floor had all the rooms open to a common outdoor walkway. It looked nothing like the picture in the brochure.

"We hopped out to register. I leaned into a hallway next to the office. As I walked closer, I could see the valley. 'Jaxie. Look at this. They took pictures of the back of the building! They even doctored those pictures. This is a scrawny valley—no mountain view, and the motel is flat. They probably used a fisheye camera lens to make it seem like a crescent.'

"We stood there shaking our heads," Nina told Phil. "Then it got worse. When we checked in, they told us all the valley-view rooms were booked, so we got to look out our window onto the parking lot. No balcony. And their elevator was closed for repair! We had to drag our stuff up the stairs. By the time we got the last box into our parking-lot-view room, I was spent—dying of thirst. I yelled, 'Hey. Throw me a bottle of water.' We looked all over. There was no drinking water in our room. Nothing! And I'm not about to drink out of the tap these days!"

Phil looked into her strained eyes and said, "Nina, I feel for you. Terrible when expectations are not met."

"Right Mr. Stone—Phil. Right, Phil." Nina grinned at him. "I may be young but I know one rule. You don't make a promise you don't intend to keep. Ever! Even worse. You don't make a promise you could never keep!" she said emphatically. "The Crescent is a perfect example. Their brochure didn't give a written promise, but it sure led to unmet expectations. Set expectations way up and miss by a mile and you piss people off, big time!"

Phil told her, "In business, if you overpromise and underdeliver, you will piss off countless people—before you go out of business. Give people more than they expect and people will love you. Underpromise and overdeliver—that's the key. It's the same in every aspect of life." Nina was breathing easier, so Phil asked, "So then what happened?"

A much calmer Nina continued. "The Bonner gives each guest complimentary bottled water. Not The Crescent. I threw on a jacket to go outside and find a vending machine. I expected to put my money in, push the button, and get my bottle of water. I pushed the button and nothing. I could hear the machine making noises, but no water. I was irritated, and getting thirstier by the minute. Admitting defeat, I pressed the coin return, and guess what?" Before Phil could answer, she raised her voice and said, "It took my money too. I got nothing!"

Nina continued, "I stormed over to their front desk and composed myself. I didn't want to be one of those people, you know, who act like the front desk people are personally responsible for everything in life. So I calmly told my story, figuring they would help. Nope. The front desk guy tells me, 'Gosh, I'm sorry, but the vending machines are supplied by an outside vendor.' I was a customer of the motel, and their machine took my money and gave me nothing. Who cares who owns that machine? It was in their motel for their guests. Shouldn't they take some responsibility? And that front desk guy didn't do anything. He could have said, 'Here's a free bottle of water,' or 'Let us refund your money.' Nothing. I was pissed off. Then I thought there might still be some water in the RV. Took me ten minutes digging through every drawer and cabinet before I finally found a bottle. I know it's not the same as our phone tree system, but I could feel the pain that lady, Jill, was living through."

Without taking a breath, Nina went on. "She heard the same menu so many times, she memorized it. Imagine how bad I felt when she told me that! Jill repeated word for word what she heard when she pressed our Guest Services button. 'Thank you for calling Guest Services. If you know your party's extension, you may dial it at any time. You may use our Voice Prompt System to efficiently route your call by telling me what you need. You can say things like, 'Bellman,' or 'Valet,' or 'Room Service.' How may I help?'

"Jill said it took so long to get any response, she had forgotten she'd chosen Guest Services on her first try, so she thought, '*It must be Guest Services that I need. I'll try saying that.*' Then, as clearly as possible, Jill slowly said, 'Guest Services.'

"A moment passed. Jill heard what she called 'clicking sounds,' and then, 'Thank you for calling Guest Services. If you know your party's extension, you may dial it at any time...' Jill told me she was done with all this and slammed her hand down on the nightstand and yelled, 'Operator!' into the phone. A moment later an actual live voice came on. 'Operator, how may I direct your call?'

"Jill thought she finally got the help she needed. Jill told the voice, 'Thank you for picking up. I have been trying to get help for my shower. It won't stop running and I'm afraid it could flood my bathroom.' Then the voice told her, 'I am not actually onsite. We are remote. Part of their answering system. But I understand. I can help. I will connect you with Guest Services. Please hold.' Without a chance for Jill to get a word in, that music started playing again. The live voice had disappeared. Moments later Jill heard, 'Thank you for calling Guest Services...'"

Nina looked into Phil's eyes and asked, "What could I say? What would you say?"

"I've got a few ideas for you, Nina. You certainly have a negative trend going on. Let me tell you what I know about phone trees. Think of what people want. Fast food, drive-through laundry service, next-day delivery, same-day delivery, packages dropped from drones into your yard—all examples of our need for speed. People demand to get what they want now! We don't like to wait in lines. We hate sitting in a crowded waiting room. We don't like taking a number and waiting our turn. We can't stand being put on hold. Those things just piss people off. You with me, Nina?"

"I couldn't agree more," she said. "If I need help with something—getting my water bottle, or anything—I need help now! I want a live person in my area—not some stranger in a call center somewhere else in the world. But even worse than that: a phone tree! So, what's your idea?"

"Let me tell you about my first experience with anything like this. Then we can brainstorm. Okay?"

Nina sat back, beginning to relax. Phil explained, "First time I saw a switchboard was when my dad took me with him to work one Saturday when I was a boy. Switchboard operators took inbound calls, listened and learned who the caller needed, and plugged them in to connect them with the phone on the desk of their party. Everybody who called got a live person before being put on hold. These operators had to take breaks. They needed time off. They had lives, so now we have automated phone systems that work non-stop. Once paid for, they cost next to nothing to maintain. With new automated systems, we get the phone tree first, then, if we are really lucky, we get a live person who might help us. Phone trees can frustrate—but they are a necessary evil. Until someone comes up with a better process, we are stuck."

Nina laughed. "I know. These days when I make a call to a business and get a live voice, I even ask, 'Are you a real person?'"

Phil shook his head, smiling. "I know you get a ton of calls at The Bonner Hotel, so an automated system does make sense. You do need one. But, hey. Remember when you told me about that hotel guest who got pissed off with your phone tree?"

"Jill?"

"Right, Jill. You told me she finally got a real live person, right?"

Nina explained, "Yeah. But our system outsources that."

Phil gave Nina a reassuring nod. "Managers hate when teammates come up with problems. If you relate a problem without offering a solution, it always sounds like whining. You need to bring this problem to Jason Bonner, but give him the solution along with the problem. You can truly impress him, and help the entire team. Most people just whine."

"So, what's the solution?" Nina asked.

Phil answered, "I don't want to get too deep here. Stop me if you get lost, okay?" Nina nodded. "I have a potential solution, but I wouldn't start with it. Why not have the calls go to your front desk when people say 'Operator' rather than having them go offshore?"

Nina's skepticism was obvious. She replied, "Sounds great, but I don't think it will work. Sometimes we get too busy. At The Bonner, it's a sin to lose a call!"

"See, that's my point! If you just start there, with the solution, someone could shoot it down, like you almost did. Once it's shot down, it's dead. Over. So, break it down. Before you even get to the problem, find out if your solution will work. Maybe start by asking about the actual procedure. How many times does a hotel guest get automated responses before getting rerouted to a live person? What triggers that? Then ask if that trigger could send the caller right to you at the front desk. Then ask if you are busy, after so many rings, could it then go to the offshore people? Ask one question at a time. Get a positive response and build on that. You will be painting a picture in Mr. Bonner's mind, and pictures help sell concepts. It's not a snapshot. You are painting that picture one brush stroke at a time, and you owe it to yourself, Jason Bonner, and the team to paint it well. This all make sense?"

Nina slowly nodded, but said nothing. Phil was looking for a strong, positive response to know she understood him. Not getting it, he explained further. "Let me simplify. Imagine I am a guest and I tell you I'm hungry. Do you immediately give me a solution? No. You don't know if your solution will work, so you ask a question to learn more. You want to know what I am thinking, right?"

"Ah. Finally. I get it! My favorite restaurant is The Angelica. It's a short drive and they have awesome Italian food. It's not cheap though," Nina said. "Before I suggest The Angelica to anybody, a hotel guest, or even a friend, I've got a couple things to sort through. Do they like Italian? I could ask, 'What kind of food are you in the mood for?' and see if my solution still fits. If not, I guess I need a new solution."

Phil smiled. He was thrilled Nina was catching on so quickly. She was not only coachable, but had a genuine hunger to learn. "You got it! You need to find out if they mind a short drive. You need to ask about the budget. Their answers will direct you to your next question. Once you are sure your solution is a viable pathway, go for it."

Phil apologized for making that sucking sound with his straw as he attacked every last drop of his smoothie, then walked Nina to her car. "Good luck with Jason Bonner. I've heard he's a good guy. Think through your plan. Imagine all the possible directions your conversation might go, and develop a way to handle each possibility. That will do two things for you: First, you'll be prepared for everything, so you are positioned for success. Second, your preparation will amplify your confidence. Any time you need to get a point across, you need unstoppable optimism. Nina, you are a very confident young woman. This will help you take that power to another level!"

Tips from the Communication Toolbox

- *Test potential solutions by reading the mind of your listener.*
- *Never overpromise and then underdeliver. Do the opposite: overdeliver and underpromise.*
- *Preparation builds confidence. Confidence is contagious!*

CHAPTER 6

PERSPECTIVES

Concepts:

Picasso was considered by many to be the father of abstract art. Ask a thousand people what they see in a Picasso painting and you will likely get a thousand different answers. Each person sees the painting from a different perspective. Look at things from different points of view— different perspectives. You will learn something new each time you do.

Nina took the reins at the reception desk. Reservations were a snap. She'd ask her questions, always making sure she kept it conversational, and even injecting some humor now and then. Little jokes always seemed to relax people. Check-out was at eleven, so the hours just before and after were hectic, but she breezed through those times. She found herself on the phone with a guest who was being difficult, pissed off about getting two double beds when they expected a king, and acting like it was Nina who personally disappointed them. Nina's apology was heartfelt, but way over the top, and Jason was in earshot and heard it all.

"Hey Nina. You seem to get a little tongue-tied when people are cranky. I can tell you really feel for people having a tough time, but you can help them best if you pick a perfect angle on your apologies. Ready for another short coaching session?" Jason asked. Nina nodded.

"Nobody is perfect, and everybody knows that. We all make mistakes. People will give you some space if they feel you honestly and sincerely want to help. The words you choose when admitting an error should fit the situation. Like Goldilocks did with the beds at the three Bears' house, pick the phrase that is not too soft, not too hard, but just right."

"Thanks, Mr. Bonner," Nina replied. "I appreciate you helping me with this. I admit, I do get uncomfortable."

"I need you to stay upbeat and instill confidence in our customers—even when they are upset. And I want you to be happy. Here's a list of apology approaches from unemotional to filled with emotion." Jason paused, and handed Nina a sheet of paper with these phrases written on it:

- *Pardon me*: no emotion.
- *Excuse me*: no emotion.
- *I apologize*: very low emotion—not personal.
- *I regret*: medium emotion.
- *I'm sorry*: high emotion—personal.
- *I beg your forgiveness*: very high emotion.
- *I'm embarrassed*: highest emotion.

"I think you'll like this, Nina," Jason said. "It's helped me, and I try to get the team to buy in by showing them how this will make their lives easier…and help others. Ready?"

"My pen is poised," she said, smiling.

"Well, 'pardon me,' or 'excuse me,' work perfectly for a minor indiscretion. These are the least personal of all on the list I gave you. These convey no emotion other than what is carried in the tone and inflection of the voice.

"Next is 'I apologize.' It implies no emotion, only the understanding that there was some kind of mistake or error. 'I apologize' is a perfect unemotional approach. Add 'truly' and inject the slightest bit of emotion, like 'I truly apologize.' You with me?"

Nina was jotting down notes on the paper Jason had given her. She looked up and said, "I'm tracking with you, but not there yet. Keep going."

"I'll tell you a funny story. At least it was for me. After the passing of Queen Elizabeth in 2022, one of her assistants was interviewed, and was asked what the Queen was really like. The interviewer recounted difficult times the Crown had gone through and asked why the Queen never actually apologized. The assistant answered with that charming English accent: 'The Queen didn't do apologies, she did regrets.' I laughed out loud when I heard that. I even wrote it down so I wouldn't forget it."

Nina smiled as she scribbled more notes.

Jason continued, "And there's more. The Queen never put the regret on herself. It wasn't, 'I regret,' it was 'We regret.' I loved that too. She used 'we' to share the blame and take herself off of the hot seat. Something to think about before you apologize. Take that target off of your back by using 'we' if it fits.

"Think about the difference between 'I apologize' and 'I'm sorry.' 'I'm sorry' is filled with emotion. It is personal. It gives the impression that you are emotionally hurt and saddened by the situation. Add 'so' to add more emotion. 'I'm so sorry.' See how that is more powerful?"

"I'm getting it, Mr. Bonner. This will help me."

"Just two more on my list. 'I beg your forgiveness,' is brimming with sympathetic emotion. It's almost like crawling to apologize. And 'I'm embarrassed,' starts an apology by putting the damaged person on a pedestal, and you in a subordinate position. Add 'so' to this phrase for a more dramatic statement. You may be dealing with a tough situation and need a more aggressive apology. Try combining those phrases, or add one more word to bring it up another notch. Add 'please.' 'I'm so sorry. I truly apologize. Please, I beg your forgiveness.' See how that multiplies the impact? Pick what fits. The apology that fits the situation best will win their acceptance of your apology. Sincerity is key. 'I'm so embarrassed. I truly apologize. I'm so sorry. Please, I beg your forgiveness!' That's over-the-top powerful. Said with tears in your eyes while on your knees, your head slightly bowed, would be even more powerful, and probably a bit ridiculous. That's what I mean. Sincerity is your target. The phrase you pick must match the situation. If you accidentally bump into someone and neither of you is hurt in any way, saying 'I'm so sorry. I truly apologize. Please, I beg your forgiveness,' is too over-the-top. A simple, 'pardon me' is fitting." Jason grinned. "If you accidentally knock the person to the ground and both bags they were carrying split open and their groceries spew out into the street to be crushed by passing cars, a simple, 'pardon me' just won't cut it. You need a strong emotion-filled response like, 'I'm so embarrassed. I truly apologize. Please, I beg your forgiveness.' Then you'd better go help salvage some groceries!"

As their laughter subsided, Jason said, "Don't expect to master this in a day. Just play with it—and not only here at The Bonner, but anytime in your life when you are consoling someone who is upset."

"Thanks, I will."

Jason reached out his hand and shook Nina's. "When your dad asked about you working here, I was hopeful and excited. I hoped for the best. But what I hope for, I don't always get. This time—looks like I did! I'm still very excited. Thanks, Nina."

Nina bowed, blushing. "I thank you, Mr. Bonner! I do have something I'd like to run by you if I could," Nina added, with a questioning tone. "Millie told me in training that she dealt with lots of cranky people, and she helped me with some ideas to smooth those interactions out. You've given me more today, but I was thinking…"

"Go ahead," Jason said. "I value your opinion. You came up with that great idea for our Customer Management System. And you see me listening to the team whenever any of you guys have ideas or concerns. It's one of my tools to help me retain good talent. I listen."

"You do make everybody feel important, and the team thrives because of that. I see it every day," Nina commented. "Well, here's my idea. Can I ask you a couple questions about our phone system here at The Bonner?"

"Sure, what's up?"

Remembering what Phil told her about bringing solutions along when you bring up problems, Nina took a deep breath and began. "Seems like people sometimes get frustrated with our phone tree, and I have some ideas."

Jason nodded. "We spent gobs of money on it, and we keep upgrading, but I know. I'm not totally happy with it either. Let's hear what you've got."

Nina smiled and asked, "When a guest calls, pressing the 'customer service' button, they go into the phone system, right?"

"Yep. And our AI gives them voice prompt options."

"And that works most of the time," Nina added. "But when guests need a live person to help, they go offshore first. Could the system give them a new option to get live help?" Nina didn't pause there because she could feel the possibility of a 'no' response from Jason, so she smoothly continued. "Instead of pushing buttons and winding up talking to a live person in another part of the world, what if the first option for live help was the front desk? The front desk can get most of those calls. I'd sure rather be their source of help when they first need it. The way it works now, those same guests get pissed off and beat me up after fighting with our phone tree. And I know…I might be super busy, and the worst thing would be to leave these guests hanging, so could we set it up where if the front desk can't grab the call, say, in five rings…then it goes to those answering folks?"

Nina was about to ask if Jason liked the idea, but then she remembered her coaching from Phil. He told her to assume Jason would like the idea. Just ask a really simple question instead. If he said 'no' to the simple question, she could try another approach. She could look for a different pathway to help Jason open up to the idea of changing the system. "If that wouldn't be too hard to reprogram, I think it would help. Do you think reprogramming would be possible?"

"Could take a couple days, but I'm sure they could do it," Jason said. "Hmm. That really is a fabulous idea."

"I knew you'd like it!" Nina said enthusiastically. Then she used a simple, alternate of choice question. "If you want, I could call them and go over these changes for you. Would you like me to get it done, or would you rather handle it yourself?"

"No, Nina. I like your idea. Can't see any downside, but how 'bout you and I get together with the programming people? Let's see if they think of something we missed, okay? But I love to see you thinking out of the box. Congratulations on such a creative idea. Well done!"

Nina seemed to glow as she walked out of Jason's office.

Later that evening Phil got a call from Doug. "Hey, my brother, gotta' thank you."

Phil couldn't think of anything he had done for Doug. "I appreciate being appreciated, but what did I do to deserve it?"

"Jason Bonner just called telling me how blown away he is by my Nina. Almost made my heart burst with pride. He told me she came up with some great ideas for their phone system and she's working directly with Jason to get it done. How cool is that?"

"Way cool," Phil said, on the edge of his seat, curiosity peaked. "So, then what?"

"So, then I called Nina, and she told me you had coached her on how to sell Jason on her idea. She did what you said—broke it down into pieces and got positive responses. Then when she was ready to ask if Jason liked the idea, she assumed he would, like you told her. When the answers to all your questions make you believe you will get a positive response if you ask a direct question, just assume the positive response and ask a simple question instead, right Phil?"

"Yep. First time I saw that was when we bought our first house. The agent showed the home and asked if we liked this, and if that was what we were hoping for—stuff like that. I knew the price. I knew we loved it. I was really interested, and as I stewed, leaning toward telling her that we'd buy it, she simply said, 'The seller will let you keep their planters in the backyard. They can go with the house if you like. Want the planters to stay, or should I have the seller take them when they move?' I looked at my wife, Kim, and asked what she thought. She said, 'I like the planters,' so I looked at the agent and said, 'We'll take the house with the planters.'"

Doug chuckled. "Nina did it just like that. She asked a very simple alternate of choice question. It worked beautifully. Jason loved the idea—and gushed about Nina. I know this will help her get past all the negativity she's been trying to navigate through. Great stuff, Phil!"

"Wow. I love when things work," Phil said, smiling with pride. He knew Doug could hear that smile in his voice. "Nina is a natural difference maker. She adds value. It helps her team and their customers, and it helps her. She really understands the concept of 'win-win,' and she's obviously learned a key point. In short, these techniques are all about helping people, not ever jamming something down their throats. Convincing using persuasion is, to me, the ultimate form of selling."

Phil could perfectly picture Doug shaking his head as he heard Doug say, "Man. With you, everything is selling. I've learned so much from you and I use that stuff, even though I don't sell products. Looks like Nina's learning too. Can't thank you enough, brother!"

Still smiling, Phil replied, "Doug, you are such a natural with your ability to ask questions, you will love this next persuasion method. It gives you direct insight into what people are thinking. Let me take another minute and give you a cute one. You have a minute?"

Doug just said, "Sure. Go!"

"When someone makes a statement or asks a question, and you know they expect your response, yet you have no clue which direction to take to find that perfect answer, you might use this technique. I call it the 'Hot Potato.' I remember when we first met, I used some sales jargon and you 'Hot Potatoed' it right back to me. I told you how impressed I was with Loretta's alternate of choice questions. It was my phrase, 'Alternate of Choice.' You didn't ask some long question or admit you had no idea what I was talking about. You 'Hot Potatoed' me. I said, 'alternate of choice,' and you wanted to know more. You wanted to understand what I meant by that phrase, so you simply asked, 'alternate of choice?' and what could I do? I had to explain what I meant."

"Wow," Doug exclaimed. "Me! I was using a persuasion method? Funny. I just had no clue what you were talking about."

"That's when this works—when you need to know more," Phil said. The best way I can explain the Hot Potato technique is to use a really simple example, a low-stakes decision. But this works with high-stakes situations too. Let's start with what I call a low-stakes decision. Say it's a Saturday. You and Loretta both have the day off. She looks at you and asks, 'You going to Home Depot?' What do you answer?"

Doug replied, "If I'm figuring on going, I'd say, 'Yes.' That okay?"

"It could be better," Phil said, without a hint of judgment. "What you really need to know is why she is asking the question. You could say, 'Why do you ask,' but that's a stiff question that could make Loretta feel like she has to justify herself. No one likes to be challenged. If you ask a question that makes someone feel they must explain themselves, you've created anxiety. Not good. There is a better way."

Phil could feel Doug taking this all in. "Maybe Loretta wants you to help her at home, so she is hoping you are not going out. Maybe she wants something at Home Depot and hopes you will pick it up at the store. Maybe she wants to go to Home Depot herself and is hoping you can go together. Maybe. Maybe. Maybe. This is not a critical high-stakes dilemma, but still… Wouldn't you like to know what answer she wants before you take a shot at answering?"

"Okay. I see what you mean. And asking Retti, 'Why do you ask?' That's like I'm interrogating her. You know Retti. She won't stand for that. So—how do I find out what she wants me to say without pissing her off?"

"You'll need to let this sink in. It's a simple concept, but not something folks are often taught. You hear examples in regular conversations all the time, but people use this more by accident than on purpose—until they truly understand it," Phil answered. "Loretta asks if you are going to Home Depot. All you say is, 'Home Depot?' and she will answer your short question with more information for you. That's the Hot Potato. Make sense?"

Doug's silence told Phil to explain further. "Okay. Picture this. She asks, 'You going to Home Depot?' and if she wants something there and you answer, 'Home Depot?' she will tell you she wants something there. You agree to get it and you are the hero. She asks, 'You going to Home Depot?' and if she wants to go too, and all you say is, 'Home Depot?' she'll respond with something like, 'What time are you going? I need to go too.' Now you get it?" Phil asked.

Doug still didn't seem convinced, so Phil explained further. "The Hot Potato is something I train salespeople on. But it's not a 'sales tactic.' People hate to be sold. They want to make their own decisions, but they do appreciate help. That's what all the techniques I live by are based on—helping people make the right choices so they get what's best for them. You learn this Hot Potato and you will own a fantastic method to learn what people are thinking."

"So Retti asks if I'm going to Home Depot, instead of answering with an answer she may not like, I ask her a question?"

"Right," Phil said. "And a simple one. Picture this. Foil-wrapped potatoes are baking in the campfire flames. I toss one to you. You'd toss it right back. You get asked a vague question and you want to give the right answer. You toss their question right back."

"I get it now," Doug said with a confident tone. "If somebody asks, 'Are you hungry,' I don't know what they want me to say. If they aren't hungry and want to skip a meal and do something else with me and I say, 'Yes, I'm hungry,' I have given them the wrong answer. I've disappointed them. Maybe they are hoping I am hungry so we can go eat. I get it. If I know what they are thinking, I can help them get what they want. If I respond by just asking, 'Hungry?' they are compelled to elaborate. That is the key, right?"

"That's a perfect analogy. Even with a low-stakes situation like that, doesn't hurt to go in gently. Here's a situation many businesses deal with that is about a customer buying or not—more of a high-stakes issue. Here is how I set up salespeople to deal with it. With newbies I would use the hypothetical question from a customer, 'Do they come in blue?' Then I'd ask them, 'What is the best way to respond?' Guess what they replied. They said, 'I don't know. Do we have blue as a color choice?' I'd tell them we don't. Then they said, 'Well if we don't have it in blue, I'd want to be honest so I'd tell them we don't have it in blue.'"

Doug was getting excited. He interrupted and said, "The Hot Potato answer to the question, 'Do they come in blue?' is simply asking, 'blue?' and letting them explain."

"Yes. That's it! The customer might have seen a picture and liked blue. Maybe they have tried to get blue and can't find anyone who has it. Maybe they hate blue and think blue is the only color we offer. Maybe. Maybe. Maybe. The Hot Potato doesn't fit in every situation, so think it through. If I toss you a foil-wrapped hot potato, you might juggle it from hand to hand before you toss it back. Toss their question around in your mind. Think it through. Then ask the question when you are sure it will get results."

Doug started to laugh. "Last week Retti decided to model a new outfit for me. As she spun around slowly in front of me, showing off, she asked a question that I took too long to answer. I couldn't think straight. She asked, 'Do I still look fat in this outfit?' I didn't know what to say. Either choice, yes or no, I'm in trouble. I couldn't think of anything. Then, with my silence, she stamped down her foot and yelled, 'I do, don't I!' and she stormed out of the room. I pissed her off! Couldn't believe it! Took me twenty minutes to get back in her good graces. She did look beautiful in her new outfit. I should have said that. Even better, I just should have used your hot potato and said, 'Fat?'"

Phil shook his head, chuckling. "Now that was truly a high-stakes situation. You are right. Hot potato could have solved it for you."

"Love it," Doug said. "You tell this to Nina yet?"

"Don't think so. Ask her."

"I will!" Doug said with such enthusiasm Phil could feel him smiling on the other end of the phone. "And if you didn't teach her the Hot Potato, I'll teach her. I'm excited just thinking about it!"

The next morning Phil got a text from Nina. It said, "Owe you one large smoothie. Meet you at noon today, or does tomorrow work better?"

Phil thought, "*Man. I wish I learned as fast as Nina Ross. Instead of asking a question I could answer with a simple 'no,' she gave me an alternate of choice question. She's quick!*"

His return text said, "Meet you at Soothie-Smoothie today at noon. Never put off until tomorrow, something I can get done today. Can't wait to see you!"

The corner booth at Soothie-Smoothie was the perfect quiet place to talk. That's where Phil found Nina. He slid off his jacket, put it on the bench seat, and sat across the table. "Great to see you, Nina. I understand you were a big hit," Phil told her. "Your dad called and said you talked with Jason about the phone system and he loved the idea. Congratulations!"

"It went just like I imagined—even better. Now I'm a hero, and I owe it to you, Mr. Phil."

Phil thought, "*She's decided calling me 'Phil' is tough for her. So, she's calling me 'Mr. Phil.' How cute!*"

"Nina," Phil replied. "I was just a coach. You were the star player. It was you who got it done—all you!"

They ordered their smoothies and chatted about nothing for a while. Then Nina looked up with a more serious look on her face. "I was talking with my dad, telling him how Mr. Bonner coached me on upselling, and Dad said I should ask you about it. He said a long time back you mentioned upselling, but didn't go into detail. I'd love to hear your take."

"Amazing!" Phil said. "Some kind of memory your dad has. I told him how your mom moved me to take two pairs of glasses when I had only planned to get one, and that was upselling. It must have been well over a year ago. How he remembered that, after all this time, I don't know. Everybody's mind works differently, I guess."

Nina agreed. "I totally get it. Jaxie and I would find our space in the RV parks, and I'd need something at the park office or maybe their laundry area. I'd have no clue how to get there. I'd ask Jaxie. She could tell me, 'Go to the end of this row, then turn right. At the third trail, go right again. Then it's on the left.' I have no idea how in the world she could do that. We go someplace once, and she knows how to navigate it like she's lived there all her life. Then we'd go into a souvenir shop, and I'd see something that would be so cute in her dorm room, and she'd look at it and say, 'I can't picture it.' It's like she has no imagination."

"Not that," Phil said. "Some people can see clearly in their mind's eye. Some can't. I have no idea how anyone's mind works but mine. Wish I could. Some people can visualize things. Some people need to touch. For others—scent resonates for them. Each person is unique. If you can figure out the way people see the world, you can use that knowledge to tailor your conversation and help them see your points clearly. Ultimately you will better help them solve problems."

Their smoothies came and Nina asked, "You always order strawberry-banana?"

"Nina. Ha! You've found one of my little idiosyncrasies. I don't try new things enough. I stick with my 'tried and true.' And I know. I miss out when I limit myself. I'm working on that. Even old dogs need to try to learn new tricks," Phil said as they both grinned. "So, what's your upselling issue?"

"I want to understand it!" Nina declared.

"By now you have figured out I'm not a 'long-story-short' guy. Let's talk about upselling. First, what does that phrase mean to you?"

Nina came right back with, "Getting people to buy more."

"Buy more?"

Nina grinned and said, "Hot Potato, Mr. Phil?"

Phil nodded with a smile, thinking her dad hadn't wasted any time explaining the 'Hot Potato' to his daughter. She went on. "When people call to book a stay at The Bonner, I ask how many days they will be on vacation. When they tell me, I ask how many of those days they intend to spend at The Bonner. For example, let's say they tell me their vacation is ten days, and they plan on being with us at The Bonner for five, I am supposed to ask them what their plan is for the other five days. Without pressure or pushing, I try to get them to extend their stay with us. I'll ask them about their day-to-day itinerary while they are at The Bonner. Sometimes I can excite them about other activities they had not discovered. I try to motivate them to stay more days with us than they originally planned. I'm upselling. Maybe I point out that all the activities they have planned will make their stay a bit hectic. If they were to add another day with us, they can have a more relaxed and enjoyable time. I find a way to offer more value than they had envisioned whenever I can. When they planned five nights and I get them to schedule six because I have offered added value for their extra time with us, I've upsold them."

"Good example," Phil said. "People might think of upselling as a bad thing. As with every other aspect of persuasion, there is no room for deceit or coercion. Upselling doesn't mean jamming things down others' throats. That pisses people off. Always find a win-win. In your breakfast room, they always ask me if I would like a coffee or a dessert.

They are upselling. I often have another coffee and a dessert, and I enjoy it. Wouldn't have if they hadn't asked. I win with the extra value they give me, and the hotel wins with increased revenue."

"Ha. I know the wait staff practices that at The Bonner. They roleplay upselling at their prep meetings," Nina told Phil.

He smiled and asked, "Ready for me to stretch your definition of upselling?"

"Let me grab my pad," she said.

"Okay," Phil said. "The traditional understanding is upselling is adding value beyond expectations for a price. Couldn't upselling be adding value beyond expectations for something other than money?"

Nina had a confused look on her face "Like what?" she asked.

"Appreciation!" Phil replied. "The return for the extra added value doesn't have to be money. Appreciation is the price paid. Let me explain. There is a lot to unpack here.

"Regular upselling is everywhere. You are convinced to buy the extended warranty you had no plan to include. You thought to buy the base model, but with some coaxing, you wind up with the premium model." Phil winked. "You go to New Vision to get a pair of glasses and walk out with two pairs. Those are the kinds of things people think of when they picture upselling.

"Let's imagine I offer to pay you to help me bring materials to my car. When you're done, maybe I ask if you can do something else for me and offer to pay you more for the added work. Is that upselling?"

Nina sat with her elbow on the table, chin supported by her right hand, as she slowly tapped her index finger on her lips, deep in thought. Then she grinned and said, "Sure. It is an example of providing more value than was expected for a fee."

"Right. It's upselling," Phil said. "Let's imagine you paint homes for a living. You agree to paint my kitchen walls for a fee. When you are done, you offer to do more work than we had agreed. You ask if I will put up a five-star review if you paint my trim too. You are providing more value than I planned by painting my trim, and I will be paying you with a great review. That was an upselling opportunity you took advantage of. I win. My trim got painted. You win with that review.

"I want to open your eyes to 'upsell opportunities.' They include selling more than was planned by the buyer. But remember—when the buyer, or the person who receives the benefit, gets more than they expected, and they pay with money, or appreciation, or a great review—anything they do beyond what they had planned, that is an example of an upselling situation. Look at it that way. Expand your understanding. You did say your goal was to understand upselling, right?"

Nina sat back and said, "Hmm. I bet I know where you are going with this. Can I take a stab at it?"

"Stab away," Phil told her.

"An upsell is when more action is taken than was originally planned. I get you to buy a dessert when you just planned on a sandwich. That's an upsell opportunity I implemented. I ask you for a little favor and you do way more than I asked, it's you who is taking advantage of an upsell opportunity, right?" Nina asked.

"Right! My lawn care guys mow my yard. Their job is to mow and blow, leaving everything looking great. They do that—and bring in the trash cans I had at the curb. What is that?"

Nina slowly shook her head. "Hmm. You pay them to mow, but you don't pay them more to bring in the trash cans."

"Are they taking more action than I expected?"

Nina nodded. "Ah. They get paid by your appreciation. They do extra and you are grateful. So, it truly was an opportunity to upsell!"

"Almost every human interaction contains an upsell opportunity. Just takes a simple act of kindness sometimes. The two of us are about to board the airport shuttle. I gesture for you to go ahead of me. I took action beyond what was expected. It's an upsell opportunity for me. You acknowledge my extra effort with a 'thank you' and a big smile. That's my payment. Most of the payment you will get when you upsell with extra effort is appreciation. You drop your scarf and I reach to pick it up for you. Upsell opportunity for me, wasn't it? Upsell opportunity—recognized and taken full advantage of! Cool?"

Nina smiled and said, "You are going to tell me to always look for upsell opportunities. I see. They are everywhere when interacting with people. Tips are a great example. I go over and above—I get a tip. Heck, even when I don't get a tip or even appreciation when I discover and implement an upsell opportunity, I get the personal gratification that I am a good person for doing good things for other people. I get it!"

"Proud of you, Nina. You are a joy to coach. I remember our family's first stay at Disney, ages ago. We were staying at The Swan Hotel. When we checked into our room there was a swan creatively made of hand towels on our bed. A feeling of joy rushed through me at the sight of it. It was a Disney upsell opportunity. They gave me more than we expected. I still remember how that felt." Then Phil asked, "Does the staff at The Bonner do anything special—over and above for guests when they prep the rooms?"

"Nothing dramatic," Nina responded. "But they make a little doily at the end of the toilet paper roll and a bow out of the hand towels. You'd call that an upsell opportunity."

Phil laughed. "Maybe I am the only person on the planet who would say it's an upsell opportunity, but that is what it is. I define it as doing something above and beyond for people. I always ask myself, 'Is there an upsell opportunity here?' Always. It might be as simple as walking through a door and then holding it open for the person behind me. Maybe just smiling and saying, 'Good morning' to a stranger."

Nina was awestruck. "Wow. Upselling. I had no idea. Imagine how different the world would be if everybody looked for upsell opportunities like that all the time. I'd like to live there!"

Tips from the Communication Toolbox

- *People like fun—and funny is. Inject humor and relax people to open them up.*
- *Be an obvious listener. People love to be heard.*

- *Every person is unique. Don't expect them to see things your way unless you take them there.*
- *Don't set personal limits by acting like an old dog that cannot learn new tricks.*

CHAPTER 7

TRANSFORMATION

> Concepts:
>
> Some things are tough to lose: money, your job, your house, your health, even a little football game. Some things are great to lose: some weight, a bad habit, or the ugly sweater you got in the Christmas Secret Santa drawing. Either way—win or lose—never lose control of your attitude. Manage it. Manage your self-image. Hold yourself in high regard. People will have to look up just to see you. And be true to yourself, and everybody else.

Nina said, "Mr. Phil. Got a question for you. You came up with a fantastic plan for me to convince Mr. Bonner to reprogram our phone system. I followed your direction and scored with it. And all the coaching you've given to my dad—that's helped him too. You would have loved how my dad explained the 'Hot Potato' to me! Can't thank you enough. I know it must be quite a story—how did you learn all these skills you've been sharing with us?"

"Not a short story. Are you good?" Nina nodded.

"Back when I started junior high, I fell in love with rock music. I saw The Beatles on TV. Thousands of young teenage girls—girls my age—were acting like these four Beatles with floppy mop hair were Gods. I came up with a simple plan. I would stay far away from any barber, and I'd beg Santa for a guitar! Ever try to master a musical instrument, Nina?"

"I took piano for a couple years. Didn't stick with it," she said.

"All instruments take patience—more than I had back then. I got so frustrated with my fingers not working right, I would quit after five minutes. Almost a year passed, and Christmas was on its way. I planned to put in my request, but as I said the word, 'Christmas,' Dad snapped—breathing fire. 'Last year you begged and begged for a guitar. Santa couldn't get it for you, so I worked a ton of extra hours to make the money to buy it. You know where I work. Wurlitzer! Bet you didn't know they make more than pianos. Wurlitzer is also the home of Harmony guitars. That's how you got it—with my time and sweat. Now it collects dust under your bed.' The more he talked, the louder and angrier he got. 'I talked with your mother. If you don't learn to play two songs by Christmas—Mom on her piano and you playing that guitar, I am going to sell it…period!'

"Dad was right. I hadn't even touched that guitar for six months. But I felt a huge loss coming. I learned the significance of 'fear of loss.' Fear of loss is a powerful motivator that moves people to action. The world of commerce is ruled by fear of loss. If you don't buy that product before the sale is over—you lose. If you don't ask your doctor if that miracle medicine you saw on TV is 'right for you'—you lose. If you have an accident and you don't use an attorney—you will certainly lose. We are programmed from an early age to worship winning. We believe we must win, and are terrified of being a loser. No one wants to lose! Fear of loss motivated me to figure out a way to not lose my guitar.

Nina was slowly nodding as she said, "Yeah. Crazy. Fear of losing can make people frantic. I can't find my phone, and I feel like life is over until I have it back in my hands. I try to remember what Mom always says when she loses something. 'We will find it, and we know where it will be—in the last place we look!' I try to think of that. It makes me smile and takes some stress away."

"That's really adorable. I can picture Loretta saying that," Phil said. "But if my dad sold my guitar, it would be gone forever—not in the last place I look. Loss can be forever. That's why losing is so scary…and such a powerful motivator!"

Nina grinned back. Phil smiled and went on. "So, Mom looked through her piano sheet music to find Christmas songs that showed a diagram of the finger placement on the guitar. She gave me six or eight songs to pick from. I chose two easy ones. The day came to prove my skills to Dad.

"Mom said, 'You are getting faster at getting those fingers in the right position. The strings are not muffled by bad fingering. Your chords sound clean. You can do this.'

"Mom's encouragement made an amazing difference. She had nothing to do with increasing my skill level. She impacted my attitude. It was a great lesson about a positive attitude and the power that comes with it. For the first time, I believed I could do it. Dad sat with a grin on his face. That too was an attitude booster. *The moment of truth,'* I thought. *'I do this right—I'll keep my guitar.'*

"I wiped my sweaty palms on my shirt. Mom sat at the piano, hands poised above the keys. 'One, two, three, four,' and we began. I was hitting the changes. Now Dad had a big smile on his face. Silent Night and Little Drummer Boy worked. No loss for me! I kept my guitar!

"There were so many lessons in my journey to learn to play. Frustration stifled me when I first tried my new guitar. I should have pressed myself to keep trying, but I did not know how to manage myself. I gave up too easily. It took fear of loss and the steaming challenge from my dad to move me to action. Self-motivation is a better option. Agree?"

"Yep. I agree. I learn more about who I am and how I react to things every day," Nina said. "Unlike a lot of people, I pay attention. The better I know my negative tendencies, the easier they are to manage. Build on my positives and overcome my negatives…Hey, you still play?"

"Not professionally anymore," Phil told her. "I used my persuasion skills, as frail as they were back then, and joined a top regional band, Jasper Wrath, as their bassist. I sang a little too. I was eighteen, and on my way to becoming a star. My first album release was with Jasper Wrath. The next was with a band I founded called Eyes. My third was with Grace Slick called *Welcome to the Wrecking Ball*. I figured I had finally made the big time. The album hit number forty-nine on Billboard international charts in 1981 and a nine-month-long European tour was scheduled for the following year. At least that was the plan.

"Some disastrous marketing mistake made by our record label ruined my music career. They ran out of money. The day after Christmas, Grace called me saying the tour was dead—canceled. Astonished and in shock, I asked, 'What are you going to do? Are you going back with Jefferson Starship?' Before she could answer I blurted out, 'What should I do? What are we going to do now?'

"I was beyond upset. After New Years I planned to connect with musicians and producers I'd met over the years and persuade my way into another major band. I knew a lot of people, true rock stars, and they knew me. But it felt like I had reached the top of the mountain, and through no fault of my own, fell off. At a holiday family gathering, I sat down and admitted my disappointment to Dad.

"I looked at him and said, 'I can't believe it. Music used to be so pure—so fun. Now it seems to be more of a business than a joy. I'm gonna' have to find another band,' I complained. 'Dad, I've listened to you grumble about corporate politics for years. Man—we should have gone into business together. You know—a father and son business.' I smiled. Dad smiled. We clinked our glasses to toast our wistful dream. I thought that was it. Boy was I wrong!

"A month flew by. I was contacting everyone I knew in the music industry, completely absorbed in my quest to find myself a new band. I heard a ding-dong and answered the door—and Dad was there...with a strange grin on his face. He came in and excitedly said, 'I did it. I bought us a business!'

"Stunned, having all but forgotten our Christmas dream, I tried to keep composed and just said, 'Great. Uh. What kind of business?'

"He proudly said, 'Alarms!' His excitement told me I had stuck my foot deep in my mouth when I made that comment about a father and son business. I hadn't been serious. Obviously Dad was.

"Confused, I asked, 'Alarms? Like burglar alarms? Like banks have? Burglar alarms?'

"He told me, 'No, no. For homes. Burglar alarms for homes.' I can still hear that obvious air of pride in his voice.

"I had never heard of anybody who had an alarm system in their house. Why would anybody need one? Maybe the rich and famous? Burglar alarms for regular homes—seemed ridiculous. Obviously, somebody had sold Dad a line of bull. What now?"

Nina said, "These days alarm systems are common. We have one at home. Lots of people do. Your dad took your idea seriously, didn't he? How'd you feel about that?"

"Awful! As much as I wanted to grab my bass and escape to another part of the world, I had said something that made Dad take serious action. He bought a business. Grandpa told me guys he worked with would make agreements to build huge apartment buildings in Chicago. They didn't spend days with attorneys scrutinizing every word in the contracts. They shook hands. That was it. Their word was their bond. I was taught to live by that rule. I hadn't actually promised Dad anything, but his action demanded my follow-through. After years of wiring guitars and building speaker cabinets, I was pretty handy, so I decided to take on the role of technician. Dad could sell.

"The package he bought included training in Charlottsville, Virginia. We went together. I'll never forget my first impression of the place. Sitting at folding tables in a classroom style conference room were a dozen sets of people who had purchased dealerships like Dad. There were groups of two people, like me and dad, and even larger groups. The training team was very impressive. The trainees? Not so much. I whispered in Dad's ear, 'Look at these people. If they can make it with their alarm businesses, we will kill it!' He smiled."

Nina said, "Sounds like you started buying into the alarm idea."

Phil nodded and said, "I was. I knew we had more going for us than those other trainees. Dad owned a house in Bridgeport, Connecticut on a pie-shaped property where Park Avenue and Brooklawn Avenue intersect. We set up shop there. Dad set appointments with referrals from all the people he knew. He even got phone numbers of burglary victims from the local newspaper. He'd get dressed in a suit and tie and spend a couple hours presenting our offerings to customers, while they would provide something to drink and a comfortable place to sit. Then he'd bring the sales order to me. My job was to get those products installed.

"Customers get anxious when a stranger knocks on their door with electric drills and saws, intending to chop up their house. So, I learned ways to keep them calm. Anxious people would follow me around, asking why I was doing this and why I wasn't doing that. They could be a pain and cause me to either make mistakes or waste a ton of time—or both. Calm customers would relax and let me do things undisturbed. I could do better work for them, and I could save both the customer and me some time.

Nina said, "Makes sense. How'd you get them to relax?"

"When I would knock on a customer's door on installation day, they would see me dressed in a work uniform with a blue button-down shirt with 'Phil' embroidered on the pocket. My hat had the company name, American Safety, embroidered on it. Both were props that were an important part of the show I would be putting on to relax these customers. Another prop was my shop vacuum. It was the last tool I would need to complete my work but I brought it in first. In my other hand, I had a clipboard with all the job paperwork, and a large drop cloth. So, can you guess why the shop vac?"

"Okay," Nina said. "I have no idea. Why the shop vac?"

"It was my trick! People would see me with the vac and the drop cloth and look over my shoulder and see a clean, white truck with our logo on the door, and think, 'Looks like these guys will do a clean job.' Then they would breathe easier—and leave me to do my work."

Nina nodded. She asked, "You figured that out yourself, or did someone coach you?"

"I guess I figured it out. Trial and error—you know. Like most things, once I understood the 'why' of it, I improved over time.

"Dad created the order in hours in the comfort of the customer's home. Then I would spend entire days crawling through attics insulated with fiberglass that would stick to the sweat on my hands and face as I ran wires. I would find myself in garages that hadn't been properly cleaned in years. Insects and spiders were everywhere. Many jobs were exhausting. I would be paid seventy-five dollars for each alarm system I completed. Dad would average a five-hundred-dollar commission with each order he sold. Didn't take me long to figure out which job I would prefer. I decided to learn how to sell.

"Our dealership package included a sales training cassette series by Zig Ziglar's brother, Judge Ziglar. He had spent years as a successful in-home salesman, starting with pots and pans, then brushes and cleaning tools, and even funeral plots. If you needed someone to sell a glass of water to a drowning man, Judge would be your guy. His cassette series was called, 'Timid Salesmen Have Skinny Kids.'"

Nina's laugh and the grin on her face inspired Phil to continue. "I studied diligently and learned the company presentation. I was ready to sell. If the *Guinness Book of World Records* had been watching me those days, my name would probably still be up there for being the only salesperson anywhere who did fifty-six presentations and sold nothing, yet didn't quit. I couldn't even get an order with my follow-up calls. I'd hear a whiny, 'Well Phil, you are a great salesman. You got us thinking about being safe. We can't thank you enough.' I would brace myself because I knew what would come next. 'But we talked with some of the neighbors who already have alarms. They have Watchguard. We've decided to go with them.'

"I learned a tough lesson. Once people made their decision, it was impossible to get them to reverse and go with American Safety. I was sending Watchguard so much business, I thought about calling to get them to pay me a referral fee!"

"How funny!" Nina said, as she excused herself and darted to the lady's room. Phil checked his phone while he waited, eager to tell her about how he turned his failures around.

As Nina sat back down, Phil began, "Margarette Germain lived alone at the end of a cul-de-sac. The hedges by her sidewalk were so tall they completely hid her front porch from street view. And there had been homes hit by burglars just a street over. If anyone needed an alarm for their home, Margarette did. I had to try a different approach if I wanted to transform failure into success.

"Margarette was attentive throughout my entire dissertation. Then I got to the siren demonstration. Instead of talking in my normal tone of voice, I brought my voice to a soft whisper. To hear me, she leaned in. 'Imagine it's the middle of the night. A burglar has targeted your home. He creeps up silently, crowbar in hand, ready to attack your front door. You are sound asleep. That burglar destroys the lock as he hauls off kicking his way into the serenity of your castle—your home. But! The moment his boot hits your door…' As I said the word 'door,' I set off the burglar alarm. Then I yelled over the blaring siren, 'It's a home invasion—your home!'

"Margarette jumped right out of her chair. When she caught her breath, I continued. I got to the end, filled out the contract, and turned it toward her as I outlined what would be included. I made sure my total focus was on the contract. My left-hand index finger pointed at the 'X' I had drawn by the signature line. In my right hand was the pen I was offering her. I lowered my head and pointed to the line for the customer's signature as I said, 'I need your okay right here.' I didn't make eye contact. I just stared at that signature line and kept pointing, not moving. Time stood still."

Nina seemed confused and asked, "Why no eye contact?"

"Good question," Phil replied. "I didn't understand it then—but I do now. It's all about directing total focus on that signature line. It's time for them to take action. Eye contact is critical as you seek to know their thoughts throughout the sales process. Once you get to the end, it's all about that final decision. In this case, the signature line. Eye contact could be a distraction for the customer. It could hurt my chances. Make sense?"

"Wow," Nina said. "This is quite a science!"

"Sure is," Phil said. "Ask your final closing question and keep quiet. I was so uncomfortable; the silence was deafening. Then Margarette abruptly got up and walked out of the room."

Nina was amazed. "What? She just left? No warning? What did you do then?"

"I had no idea what to do. Did I offend her? Should I pack up my materials? Those training tapes didn't say anything about a situation like this. I could feel beads of sweat building on my forehead. I was paralyzed. Then, suddenly she reappeared. Still in shock, I had no words. But she did. She broke that silence by saying, 'Who do I make the check out to?'"

Nina laughed. She said, "What a rollercoaster ride you were on. Then what?"

"You're right. First it was nervousness. That became fear. The tension was awful. Then, next minute I had to find a way to control my euphoria. Fifty-six times I failed. No more. The streak was over—as long as I could keep it together, complete the paperwork, and gracefully pack up. She filled out the check, signed the paperwork, and held the door as I carried my materials to my car. I could hardly contain my excitement, but I knew I had to stay cool. She had no idea she was my first customer. I bit my lip as I loaded up the car. Once out of sight of her house, I let out a scream of joy that I'm sure the entire world heard.

"That same week I met with Nick and Ginny. They sat at their kitchen table listening to my presentation, paying close attention. I realized I should have practiced to the point I knew what was on every page. When I turned a page, I was so intent on making sure I read what was on it, I didn't get the benefit of seeing their facial expressions. I was concentrating on the page, not the people. Big mistake. I had no idea what they were thinking. And I didn't ask one question to find out. Another big mistake. I kept blindly marching on.

"It was time to set off the alarm. I set the stage as I had done with Margarette. As I said the word 'door,' I let it roar. Then I yelled over that blaring siren, 'It's a home invasion—your home!'

"With over-the-top excitement in my voice, I asked, 'And what would that burglar do?' I didn't stop to let Nick and Ginny answer. I kept talking. 'He'd run!' They both nodded, so I felt they were with me, and I kept talking. I got to the end of my presentation, filled out the contract, turned it, and pointed to the signature line while offering my pen. Just as with Margarette, I said, 'I need your okay right here,' and I stared at that signature line, enduring that awfully painful silence.

"Again, time stood still. I wanted to look up at their faces, but those Ziglar tapes told me to avoid eye contact and stay patient, however long it took. Neither of them uttered a word. At least neither of them got up and left the room. But my confidence was eroding—slipping away. I could feel my anxiety growing exponentially as moments passed. I felt hurt—wounded. I started questioning everything. Why was I here anyway? Why was I dealing with this torture? Maybe I should quit even trying to sell. How did I get myself into this mess in the first place? I'm a musician, not a salesman. My mind was racing down a stream of negatives. It was horrible.

"Then, out of nowhere, Nick said, 'If you can get it installed before the end of the month, we'll go with it.' Again, I was saved!"

Nina grinned and shook her head as she said, "Amazing. Twice in the same week you prevailed after all that failure. Bet you learned a ton from just that week alone, didn't you?"

"Right! I sure did! I always thought I was a born entrepreneur, but I realized I was not a born salesman. Maybe nobody is. I didn't know how, but I would have to learn why things worked and how to be persuasive to become an accomplished salesman. The title of the Ziglar tapes, 'Timid Salesmen Have Skinny Kids,' was comical, but unfortunately, there is a lot of reality in that title. I owed it to myself and my family to figure this out. My first goal: To learn methods that would allow me to sell without the pain of failure, or pissing people off by being one of those pushy salespeople everyone hates. My second: If those methods worked selling products, they should work all the time. They should work when I try to get a point across about anything—with everyone—all the time. That realization alone changed the course of my life. I made a decision to use those same principles and techniques to improve the quality of my everyday life, and to practice and hone my skills—ultimately helping myself and lots of other people.

"Selling isn't a bad thing. Selling is convincing. I like convincing. Every time I convince someone about anything, I have sold them. I sold my folks on getting me that guitar. Dad sure sold me on learning those two songs. In music, I sold myself to get in the band, and the band sold itself to our audiences with every note of every song. Trying to convince someone about virtually anything is selling. You get them to agree with you and you have sold them.

"Some sales are easy. If my hands are full and I need help opening a door and a stranger walks up, I can ask 'Would you be kind enough to open that door for me, please?' Asking people if they will be 'kind enough' is very powerful. People want to be kind. If the stranger opens the door, the sale is made. It's about moving people to take action.

"The courtship process is all about selling yourself. For many people, it is the biggest sale of their lives! But it is selling, and it is totally natural. That is how we wound up with billions of people on this planet. Everybody sells! I decided to devote the time and effort needed to learn the how's and why's of persuasion. I dedicated myself to becoming a master at selling. That is how my true journey into the art of persuasion began."

"Wow!" Nina marveled. "What a story. I am so glad I asked!"

"I'm glad you did too!" Phil told her. "The genuine interest you show makes it a joy to share the techniques I've learned with you!"

Tips from the Communication Toolbox

- *With fear of loss, you can move the immovable.*
- *If you do find what you lost, it will be in the last place you look.*
- *A bad attitude can doom you to failure, just as a positive attitude fuels success.*
- *Honor your commitments.*
- *Clearly explained benefits result in empowered action.*
- *Concentrate on the people, not just the message.*

CHAPTER 8

ASSUMPTIONS

> Concepts:
>
> Assumptions are the quicksand of life. When you find yourself in it, sometimes you can struggle and get out. Sometimes you get swallowed up. Best approach is to ask questions so you know the other person's thoughts. That's how you avoid the quicksand of assumptions in your communication. If you do suddenly realize you are about to make an assumption, at least avoid the negative and choose the positive.

Nina started at The Bonner in September when things were rather quiet. As the holiday season crept up, things changed. But the more hectic things got, the more confident Nina became.

One day, Nina picked up the house phone and saw the extension was Mr. Bonner's. "Hey Nina, it's Jason. Can you pop into my office for a minute?"

"Yes, Mr. Bonner."

She walked in and sat in the chair in front of his desk. "It's been less than six months since you started but you have excelled. The team is incredibly proud of you. Never thought about replacing her, but with our Reservations Manager leaving, we had a meeting before you got in this morning. I threw out an idea," Jason said.

Surprised, Nina said, "Oh gosh. I'm sorry I missed it. I truly apologize."

"Haha. There you go. Using your training. Love it. But nothing to apologize for. I had the meeting to test an idea. I asked the team what they thought about you being promoted to Reservations Manager." Jason remembered. He looked for a question in Nina's eyes. He watched body language to read her reaction. He saw the beginning of excitement! So, he said, "They all loved the idea—how about you? Like the idea too?"

Nina's eyes lit up the room! Jason continued, "Many things you are already doing, you will still do. But you remember when you got stuck with a guest who is booking a stay, or an event room? You would transfer that call to the Reservations Manager. She, and now you, will take those calls a step further. The questions you have learned to ask will stay the same, but you will now have to perfect a new persuasion technique. Seek reasons why a caller might book with us, and reasons they might not. Then you can base your talking points on those reasons.

"Let's imagine a weird one. Guy calls and asks if we have a helipad. How do you answer?" Before Nina could respond, Jason continued. "You could use that cute 'Hot Potato' thing your dad told me about. You could just ask, 'Helipad?' and see what he says." As Nina opened her notepad, Jason asked, "What if the guy only says, 'Yeah, a helipad. You know. Where helicopters take off and land.' You have to come up with something, but you don't know what the ultimate objective is. What is this guy looking for?"

Nina said, "I really don't know what he wants. If I assume, I risk making an ass out of him and me," she giggled, but then got serious. "One thing I have figured out. If I don't know something, I try my best not to assume. I ask questions so I go in the right direction."

"Perfect!" Jason said. "So, let's pretend I'm the guy and let's roleplay, okay?" Nina nodded. "Ring, ring, ring," Jason said.

"Thank you for calling The Bonner Hotel. My name is Nina. How may I help you?"

"Got a question for ya'. Do you guys have a helipad?" Jason asked, playing the role of a caller.

Nina confidently replied, "I'm happy to help. Were you hoping to land here, or are you looking for a sightseeing helicopter tour?"

Jason smiled. "You've got it, Nina! Well done! You start by helping them feel at ease. Whatever their question, however absurd it might be, you start by accepting what they say. You did that by saying you were happy to help. That would be reassuring. They would see you as someone who will help them." Jason paused and said, "Then you test possible solutions with a simple question. Your alternate of choice, 'Would you like this or that,' was perfect. You led them to tell you more. When they do, you will know what they are thinking, and you can choose the perfect next step in your persuasion. See, you are persuading them."

"Persuading them?" Nina asked.

Jason laughed. "Hot Potato? Yes, persuading them to book a wonderful stay here at The Bonner."

"I really do get it, Mr. Bonner. And the moment I offered those two options; I would jump online and search. I know Reno has a tour company that flies helicopters. I've never taken a helicopter tour, so while the caller is answering, I am looking for the tour company's online ratings and other info I can offer the caller. If he wants to land here, I can research what he has to do to land at Bonner Airfield. I want to be ready with solutions, no matter what direction he goes."

"Right. You are looking for reasons why the caller might book with us, and reasons why they might not. If he's looking for a helicopter tour, and you just say we don't have one here, or if he wants to land, and you tell him we have no facility, chances are we lose him. He does not book. Taking that tour or landing—both are reasons why he might not book. We have to nibble away until those negative reasons disappear. First, we need to know specifically what he is looking for. Then we ask more questions to see if one of our potential solutions will work. At the same time, we are looking for reasons why he might book, and we are building on those positives. Grow the positives and make the negatives disappear."

Nina jumped up. "Talk about timing," she said. "I hear my extension ringing. Might be a potential booking."

Nina ran and grabbed the call on the fourth ring. "Thank you for calling The Bonner Hotel. My name is Nina. How may I help you?" Nina answered with professionalism and an upbeat attitude, working to schedule a reservation.

"I'm John Hope, Nina. I was on your website and have a bunch of questions."

"Mr. John Hope, I will be delighted to help you. Would you mind a brief, less than one-minute hold?" Nina asked, buying herself a little time to gather her thoughts. Nina had listened intently to every word John Hope uttered. She asked herself, "*What can I find in his short statement that I can use to direct the conversation? Did he give any clue about reasons why he might and reasons why he might not book a stay?*" Replaying the call in her mind, she thought, "*He was on the web site. He went through the effort to make the call to the hotel. He has more than one question. He seems more than just curious. These are all reasons why he might. His questions could become reasons why he might not, negatives, depending on what he requires.*"

"A bunch of questions? I'll be delighted to help you, Mr. Hope."

"Call me John."

Nina thought, "*That's a slight positive. Personal, not formal. If John does not like me, he will be unlikely to book a hotel stay. If he felt uncomfortable, he would not give permission to use his first name.*"

John continued, "I'm an avid skier and my wife and I are planning to get away this fall…"

Nina fist-bumped the sky and thought, "*Yes! Just got a huge reason why he might. Skiing our mountain trails, hiking, kayaking, and fresh mountain air are what The Bonner Hotel is famous for. By late fall, snow covers the mountains. The Bonner is known as a quiet, intimate, couples and family destination close to nature with endless outdoor activities. I can build on that!*"

And John went on, saying, "My wife and I die for gourmet cuisine. How are your restaurants?"

Nina thought, "*Oh boy, there's my first real reason why he might not. The Bonner Hotel has a top-class breakfast room. That is it. There is no lunch or dinner served in the hotel. If I directly respond saying we offer a world-class breakfast and nothing more, that could be the end of my hotel booking.*

Nina was racking her brain searching for pathways she could try. She knows that Reno and Lake Tahoe are both within driving distance and there are countless restaurant options, but she doesn't know if John will accept the drive. Maybe he is looking for a hotel with fine dining on property.

"Restaurants, there are plenty. Tell me, will you folks be renting a car while you are here?"

Nina is testing a pathway. If John says they plan to rent a vehicle, Nina could suggest a short and breathtaking scenic drive to their gourmet meal. That would change the reason why he might not—into a reason why he might go ahead and book a stay at The Bonner. If they don't intend to rent a car, she could ask about their experiences with a ride service like Uber. She will try that pathway if needed.

"We plan to book an SUV with four-wheel drive. I know there can be some serious snow that time of the year," John says. "My wife and I want to do a bit of exploring while we're there too."

As Nina listened, looking for reasons John might book a hotel stay, and looking for reasons why he might not book, she thought through John's comment about renting an SUV and doing some exploring. She smiled. Nina learned from John's answer that the vehicle and a little driving will not be a reason why he might not. No negative here anymore—no obstacles in that pathway that she would have to address. Though Nina has yet to ask, it seems it will be just John and his wife. If they plan on skiing, eating great food, and exploring, they may be booking a long stay. All great reasons why they might—all positives for Nina to build upon.

"We serve a great gourmet breakfast here. Then, in town, just a couple miles away, are some fantastic family-style and gourmet restaurants. Within twenty minutes you'll find dozens more. I will arrange to have some of their menus available when you folks check in, sound good?"

"Yep, sounds great! Tell me…"

Nina got the booking by building on the positives John gave her as they talked. She tactfully eliminated any negatives she recognized, while not only concentrating on the words being said, but also what she could learn by reading between the lines. She fully understood the value of looking for, and then using both the positives and the negatives when booking a hotel stay. So many people ignore the negatives. And she was finally having real fun helping The Bonner's clientele.

Months passed. Jason Bonner's voice came over the intercom. "Nina Ross, please stop in my office." She came in, sat down, and opened her notepad. "Nina, since we gave you the title of Reservations Manager, you have increased the percentage of people who call and actually go beyond questions and book with us. Great job! And our average length of stay is a full day longer than before you took on the job. We know your skills on the phone contributed to that too. You helped the team navigate through the holidays, and we even got more five-star reviews than normal. Bottom line? You are improving our bottom line! It's obvious!"

Nina sat silently in the chair in front of Jason's magnificent office desk. He stood up, came around from behind the desk, and casually sat on the front corner. With his voice just above a whisper, he said, "Your dad and I came up with a timeframe before I hired you. Doug and I agreed The Bonner would have you for at least a year. Well—it's coming up soon." He paused, and then asked, "You are happy here, right?"

"I love it. It was scary at first, and I had a tough time with demanding guests, but I'm good with all that now. Yeah. I am happy. Why?"

"If you go to college in the fall—I know that's the plan—what would you do when you graduate?"

"Not sure. I haven't thought that far out," Nina answered. "But I plan on a Business Major. I've sent out applications for the fall semester."

"Sounds perfect for you. And when you get that Business Major, you'll look for a job?"

"Uh, I suppose."

Jason sat there, slowly nodding his head, lost in thought. Like surfing the web for solutions, he was straining to find the perfect pathway he could use to move Nina to be open to what he thought was an absolutely incredible idea. "Okay. And would you want to work near Bonnerville, or would you move away?"

"Geez. You've got me thinkin'. I like being around my family. Used to be scared of my dad, but he's become a buddy. And Jaxie plans to stay in town. I ever introduce you to her? She's an only child. So am I. We've been friends all through school. She's my best friend ever."

"Best friend? No. Haven't met her yet," Jason said. "But it sounds like you have a bunch of reasons to build a career in Bonnerville. Where would you work? You could work at your mom's optical place. I don't picture you at the firehouse. What other choices do you have?"

"Ah, maybe at Allworld Insurance. But not with my mom. Not my kind of place. Too small. Hmm. Not really sure," Nina said.

"Imagine this," Jason said. "Imagine you never worked here, and you graduated college. Would you consider applying for a position at The Bonner?"

"Well, sure!" Nina enthusiastically responded.

"Well, great!" Jason said, as he started to chuckle. A grin snuck onto his face. The chuckle grew into a full laugh as he playfully said, "You've already got that job at The Bonner. We've saved you four years—and probably thousands of dollars!"

They both laughed out loud as Jason sat back in the chair behind his desk. "No. Seriously, Nina. We want you here at The Bonner. Let's make that Reservations Manager job of yours permanent! Say 'yes' and I'll get you a strong bump up in pay too." Jason could see stress building. Nina looked so serious. Her normal smile had vanished. So, Jason tried to relieve some pressure. He said, "I don't need any commitment now. Relax. Think it over. Run it by your folks; I don't want you to feel even a hint of pressure. We've got time to figure this out. Give it some thought. Take your time."

Stunned, Nina gathered her things and headed for her Mustang. Her mind was spinning. Every muscle in her body seemed to tighten. Normally when she had a dilemma, she could get her dad's sympathetic ear, or her mom's logical coaching, but not this time. The idea of staying at The Bonner and not having to worry about college was incredibly exciting to her. Running the idea by her parents and trying to convince them to let her skip college scared her to death. She was lost in her own thoughts, her stress level exploding.

"I need Jaxie," she thought.

Nina made it a habit to stay positive—about everything. She figured it was her choice to allow herself to get angry or frustrated. If she could make the choice, and negative feelings always ruin a day, why not choose positive? It was not always easy, but was always worth the effort to keep on a positive path—every time.

Not now. Not being faced with telling her folks she would stay at The Bonner and skip college. If she wanted to avoid an explosion at home, maybe her only choice was to forget about the job at The Bonner. But that idea was unacceptable. She wanted that job! Confusion overwhelmed her. She couldn't create a plan. She grabbed her phone and dialed. There was no ringing sound. It went straight to voicemail.

"Hi, this is Jaxine Jackson. I can't get to my phone right now…" Nina sat there in her car. She felt so overwhelmed; she couldn't get up the strength to even start her car. She just sat there in her silence as tears welled up in her eyes.

She tried Jaxie's phone again and was even more distraught when the call went to voicemail a second time. "*Get a grip!*" she said to herself. "*Gotta figure this out. First home? Ah—can't go home and face Mom and Dad right now.*" Moments passed. Nina began to feel irritated that she had this problem. She let out a scream. "Ah! Why me? How did I get myself into this mess? Ah!" Anger crept into her being and clouded her mind. She couldn't think straight. She needed help. She felt like a dark energy was controlling her.

She started the car, backed out, and screeched out of the parking lot at The Bonner, not knowing where she would go next. Then a plan came to her. "*Hell with this. I'm driving to Jaxie's dorm. It's just an hour away. Hope she's there. It's worth a shot. I need her!*" Nina's Mustang raced up the entrance ramp for the highway to Jaxie's.

The hour-long drive seemed like days. She finally arrived. From the parking lot, Nina could see light shining from Jaxie's third-floor dorm window. A feeling of relief swept over her as she ran up to the entrance intercom. "Jaxie, it's Nina. Buzz me in?"

"Nina? Is that you? What are you doing here?"

"It's me. Buzz me in?"

Jaxie opened her dorm room door to find Nina there, no smile on her face. "Oh Nina!" Jaxie said as she hugged her buddy.

In a strained whisper Nina said, "I couldn't get you. You didn't pick up, so I came here. You didn't pick up!"

Jaxie needed to calm her friend. "Oh, I'm really sorry, Nina. I zoned out to study. My roommate is away for a long weekend so it's just me. Are you okay?"

Her voice quivering, she said, "No. I'm upset. And I am pissed off at myself. I can't stand it!"

"What? What?" Jaxie was obviously very concerned. "Here. Sit down. They won't let us cook in here, but I can make tea. Take a breath. Whatever it is, we'll figure it out. We always do." Jaxie smiled and grabbed her friend's hand with a reassuring squeeze.

Nina took a deep breath and sat on the corner of the bed. Her voice still shaky, she began, "It's about Mr. Bonner and me and staying there."

Jaxie took control. "Nina. Nina. I got you. Chill. What about staying there? You have some kinda' fight or something? What happened?"

As Jaxie poured tea, Nina just sat there quietly. Then she said, "Mr. Bonner offered me the permanent position of Reservations Manager, and more money if I commit."

"That's awesome! What's the problem?"

"That's the end of any college for me. My folks will kill me. You know how hard it was just to get our trip to happen. That was only for the summer." Nina paused and shook her head. "I just don't know what to do."

"I do!" Jaxie proclaimed. "It's popcorn and a movie. I can pop some up on this hot plate. Here. Stuff this towel over the crack at the bottom of the door. Don't want the whole floor to know I'm breaking rules." She chuckled. "Let's forget about this for tonight. Fire up the remote. Let's find a romance flick." Nina smiled for the first time. "You bring your overnight bag?" Jaxie asked.

"Gee. No. I didn't plan anything. I needed you!"

"Don't worry. I've got plenty. We're still the same size," she said as she smiled back.

The next morning Nina was still feeling beat up. She sat in silence drinking morning tea.

Just then Jaxie's phone rang. The caller ID showed it was Douglas Ross. Jaxie whispered to Nina. "It's your dad. Be really quiet." Then she answered the call. "Hello?"

"Jaxie. It's Doug Ross. Nina didn't come home from work last night. I called Jason Bonner, and he told me she left work at five. We were pretty sure she was with you, but your phone went right to voicemail.

Hers did too—still does. It was late, but Nina finally sent a text last night saying she was staying with you. No explanation. Everything okay?"

"She's here, Mr. Ross. We got caught up in a movie. She's here. She's in the bathroom. She's fine."

Doug said, "Must have been a great flick." He laughed. "I know Nina. She can get absorbed in things and get sidetracked. Wish she would have let us know a little sooner." Doug stopped his kidding and got more serious. "She texted she was with you—but didn't say why—nothing." He paused, and softly asked, "I'm guessing this was more than just a movie, right? This have anything to do with The Bonner?"

Not knowing the best thing to say, Jaxie simply asked, "The Bonner?"

"Yeah. We were expecting her home from work, but she didn't show. I called her and she didn't pick up, so I got a hold of Jason. He's a great friend. I'll bet I know what this is." Doug paused. "He told me he offered a nice raise if she stayed at The Bonner, and instead of being excited, she got stressed out. It bothered him."

Jaxie gave a little 'thumbs up' and motioned to Nina to come pick up the phone. "Daddy?"

"I just texted your mother that you are fine and with Jaxie. We were a bit concerned when you didn't come home from work, and no phone call. Not like you. I was going to ask why, but I bet I've got it figured out. I called Jason hoping I'd find you were just working late." The phone line stayed silent until Doug finally said, "Listen, honey. Jason told me he offered you a raise and a permanent job being Reservations Manager. When he told me, I thought it would be great. You were afraid to tell us, right? You thought Mom would put her foot down and make you go to college, didn't you?"

"You guys wouldn't? You and Mom both went nuts when I dropped out of scouting. When I stopped my piano lessons, you guys forced me to stay with them. You both acted like it was the end of the world when I finally quit for good. It was just piano. I hated it, but it was just piano. This is college!"

"No. You're forgetting. Remember—it was college…or a job! Hopefully a job leading to a career. Either or—college or job! We want you to be healthy, safe, secure, and happy. That's what kids get out of college—four years to figure it all out. You've got it figured out already! We are thrilled with all you have accomplished. It was a bad assumption, thinking we'd trash your idea. Bad assumption."

"Geez. I know. I can see that now," Nina said as she regained composure. "Our Ethics teacher, Professor Magle, used to say this corny thing about assumptions. Some old movie with Samuel L. Jackson he'd quote. I remember because of Jaxie. Get it? Jaxie Jackson and Samuel L. They are both Jacksons! Anyway, Samuel L. said something about when you make an assumption, you make an ass out of you and umption."

Doug laughed. "It's supposed to be when you assume, you make an ass out of you and me. You're supposed to underline those letters as you say it—pretty cute. But it sounds to me like you went through a bunch of hell with your assumption. Do me a favor?"

Nina's voice found a normal tone. "Sure, Dad. Can't believe I fell into the assumption trap again."

"Make yourself a promise. Don't assume the worst when something comes up. Don't assume the best either. Be aware of what the worst might be, and plan to overcome it. Be aware what the best might be, and plan how you might handle it if something goes wrong. Mentally prepare for all the possibilities, then ask tactful questions to figure out your next move."

Nina hung her head. "I was assuming the worst. I see. I was afraid…"

"Fear of failure is a killer. It's almost a guarantee of failure, just believing it. You know how to deal with it?"

"I do. Work through all the possibilities. Practice. Heck, Jaxie and I did exactly that with you one time, remember?"

"Yeah. You two sold me on that awesome summer road trip. Glad you did." Doug said. "See, it works."

Nina thought for a moment. "Okay. If I am reading this right, and correct me if I'm not, I have your blessing to stay at The Bonner? Mom's too?"

"Haha. That's the positive assumption you can use to see if you are on the right track. Stay positive and ask positive questions."

"So...?" Nina asked.

"I talked to Retti after Jason told me. We're so proud of you."

"So...?" Nina asked again, more emphatically.

"So, congratulations! Enjoy your raise in pay, Reservations Manager!"

Tips from the Communication Toolbox

- *In all situations, identify both the positives and the negatives, and prepare for them all.*
- *Accept what people say. Agree—even when you don't. Avoid conflict.*
- *Watch out for assumption traps. They hide out there everywhere. If you do step in one, choose the positive assumption—not the negative one.*
- *If you are expecting to fail, you are offering failure your blessing. Don't.*

CHAPTER 9

BENEFITS

Concepts:

WIIFM. No, that's not the call letters of a radio station. It's an acronym. **What's In It For Me**? If you want to move people to action—even just to change their minds, they need to clearly see how they will benefit. They need to understand why and how things will be better for them if they accept your position.

If you are a mandate person—a mandator—I know how you feel. Lots of mandators felt that way when they heard about WIIFM. They were hesitant to change. But they found mandates must be made again and again. When people understand the benefits of anything, they become 'sold' and internalize the idea.

HOW TO NOT LOSE FRIENDS AND FIGHT WITH OTHER PEOPLE

Doug got off that call with Jaxie and Nina feeling drained, but relieved. The situation with Nina was over. He was excited she would become the Reservations Manager at The Bonner Hotel. What a great beginning for her career! But now his mind returned to his ongoing dilemma at the firehouse. He was questioning his leadership skills, and a solution evaded him. Then he got an idea. He grabbed his phone and called Phil.

Phil's caller ID showed Douglas Ross was on the line. Phil smiled as he excitedly picked up. "Hey Doug. Whatcha' got?"

"Hey Phil, my brother! Hope you are well. Let me jump right to it, okay?"

"Sure. Jump. You need something?" Phil asked. "I'm always happy to help."

"Yeah, I could use your sales help on something. When I got promoted to fire chief, I knew I had to build a team. But I've had problems."

"Problems?" Phil questioned. Before Doug could answer, Phil asked, "How 'bout I buy you a coffee at The Bonner? Meet you in thirty?"

Doug took a deep breath. "Knew I could count on you. Meet you there."

It was a crisp morning with frost on everything. Doug came into the breakfast room and headed to the fireplace to warm up. Nina must have seen him come in. She ran up and hugged him. "Hey Daddy. You good?" she asked.

"Yeah. I'm good. I'm meeting with Phil to go over a business situation. I'll catch you on my way out, okay?"

Nina waved to Phil and went back to her desk. Doug took off his uniform jacket and scarf and sat down. Phil began, "Let's hear it. Let's solve that problem. So?"

"I just attended a Fire Council meeting, and they went over expected retention numbers. Mine are low. I need to figure out why. I've had people I would swear would re-up, but they don't. They quit."

"Any idea why?"

Doug put his hand on his face, pulled at his chin, head down, for what seemed like minutes. When he looked up, Phil could not only see but he could feel Doug's frustration. "I have worked here for years, and the old chief didn't have people quit. I do."

"There you go. Something changed!" Phil said, as if he'd found the secret. Then he asked, "Other than you being promoted—what else changed? Anything?"

"No. Nothing," Doug said, shaking his head slowly from side to side.

"If your people are not re-upping, and it's a consistent problem, it is a negative trend worth killing. I'm guessing you are a different leader than the old chief. Have you thought about that—about you having a different management style? Could that be it?"

Doug's forehead tightened. He was feeling incapable. "I never thought about my management style. When I ran the department as a team leader, I worked with the team every day. Now I oversee things. I give direction. I'm out doing public relations all the time. PR is a big part of a chief's job. I don't get to break a sweat with the team anymore."

"You give direction? Hmm." Without really expecting an answer, Phil continued, "So you tell people what to do? How do they take it?"

Doug exclaimed proudly, "They do it!"

"And are they sold on what you want them to do?"

"What do you mean?" Doug asked.

"Do they clearly see the value to themselves and the team? Do they see how it benefits everyone if they follow your direction? Are they sold on what you are asking them to do?"

"Geez—I never thought about it that way. I try to run things like a well-oiled machine. I've been trying to channel my dad and his tour in the US Navy. Man, that was a well-oiled machine. My dad had story after story. With discipline, they say, 'Jump,' and you jump. You don't ask, 'How high?' You jump as fast and high as you can. Things get done. That's what I've been trying to do here," Doug explained. "I have my biggest high drop-out percentage with my trainees."

"I think I can help—as long as you let me. Can I just ask a few things without you feeling defensive? Can I coach you up a little?"

"I'm listening," Doug said.

"What's your favorite sport?" Phil asked.

"I like 'em all. Favorite? Football!" Doug said, wondering where this was going.

Phil jumped in. "Okay, when a team's not performing well—defense letting runs through, passes not covered, penalty flags costing them, and they have a new coach—you ever hear a sportscaster say, 'Looks like the players haven't bought into the new system.' That sound familiar?" Phil asked.

"Yeah. Sure does," Doug confidently replied.

Phil smiled. "Said another way—the team is not sold yet, right? If the team was sold, the players would be performing better!"

Doug clenched his fist with this enlightening idea. "Yeah, I see. If they are not really sold on what to do and how to perform in the new system, the new system won't work. To expect them to really do it right, they have to believe it. They have to understand it. They need to be sold on it. I get it!"

Phil winked, nodded, and said, "You can't take a strict military approach here. Outside of the military, people need to be sold on what you ask them to do. They need to buy into the plan. People need to believe in what they are doing." He paused, and comically added, "Nice if the people in the military were sold on what they are ordered to do too."

Doug laughed.

Phil continued. "And it's not just with business. It's with everything. If you want to move people to action on anything, they need to clearly see the benefit they are going to get out of it."

Doug pulled a little notebook from his pocket. "You taking notes?" Phil asked.

"Yeah. You're giving me some great ideas."

His comment brought a smile to Phil's face. Then Phil thought of a pathway that might help him help Doug. "When Nina was little and you wanted her to be safe and not play with plastic bags, did you mandate or sell her?"

"I just told her not to play with plastic bags."

Phil didn't want to correct Doug. That might feel threatening, so he eased in. "That would be an order, a mandate. But I bet you didn't just stop there, did you? You tried to sell her on not playing with the bags. You knew if she understood the danger, she would be safer, so you sold her, right? If you only said, 'don't,' she might have played with the bags anyway."

Doug nodded as he jotted things in his notebook.

"You ever tell her, 'No more candy,' when she went bouncing off the walls with a sugar high? Did she eat more candy anyway?" Phil asked.

Doug nodded and said, "Yep. I'd always need to point out how she'd feel sick if she kept gorging on candy. And I had to remind her how she'd feel disappointed tomorrow if all the candy was gone. I really was selling her, wasn't I?"

Phil sat back, took a breath, and watched Doug feverishly scribble in his notebook. When he paused and sat back in his chair, Phil went on, "Now let's unpack this trainee dropout issue. Is there any trend going on here? Do they always quit tied to some event or is it more random, like at any time trainees might quit?"

Doug thought for a moment and said, "My worst dropout time is around the Tower Challenge."

"You guys have a Tower Challenge? What's that all about?" Phil asked.

"Yeah. The end of their level-one training we have the trainees scale a ten-story tower. We call it the Tower Challenge. The trainees attack a staircase and race up ten floors with gear weighing over forty pounds and carrying fifty feet of fire hose weighing another twenty pounds. Years ago, I did the exact same thing in my training. No problem. It wasn't easy, but I never ever thought about quitting. Me? I lose people right there!"

"Their objectives are clear? They know the goal?" Phil asked.

"Pretty simple," Doug said. "They make it to the top with all their gear and they pass. They don't make it—they fail. Some quit before they even start. Others struggle…and quit!"

"Yep. Pretty simple. You aren't quite that blunt with them, are you?"

"What do ya' mean?" Doug asked.

Phil explained, "Attitude is so important, especially when you are being tested. Do you think these trainees start their climb with confidence? Are they sold on their ability to make it all the way to the top? If not, that's your key to fixing it."

Doug pulled his notebook from his jacket pocket and started writing again. It was exciting for Phil to see Doug's passion. Enthused by his interest, Phil went on. "The way I see it, you have a couple sales to make. They need to be sold on their ability to make it. If they see that tower as an insurmountable obstacle, it will be exactly that—insurmountable. When you did your climb years ago, did doubt stifle you? No. Somehow you were convinced, sold, that you could do it. How'd that happen?"

"The old chief was a pretty inspiring guy."

"So his inspiration gave you confidence?"

"Yeah. None of us doubted we would make it," Doug said.

He sat there silently as a frown grew on his face. "I'm doing it wrong!" he exclaimed.

"Hey Doug. Give yourself some space," Phil directed. "You were doing your best, right?" Doug nodded. "Well, we just have to make your best get a little better. If you've got a few minutes, I'd be happy to help you outline an inspiring approach for your next training group, okay?"

"Absolutely!" Doug enthusiastically replied.

"Okay. First let's deal with their believing they can do it. Did the old chief call it the Tower Challenge?"

"Huh. He didn't. We called it Tower Day back then. Huh. You think what we call it is important?"

"I know this is a little over the top, but try this. If you had two choices and you wanted to pick a name that inspired the trainees and gave them confidence, would you call it 'Death by Tower' or 'Tower Day?'"

Doug started laughing. "Right. 'Death by Tower.' That'd scare 'em—and—it would send the wrong message!"

"That's my point," Phil said. "Instead of a name that is intimidating and promotes fear, try a positive one like Master the Tower Day, or if you want to steal a name from the past, Tower of Power Day. That's a start. I'd bet these trainees are in the very best shape of their lives by the time this test is dumped on them. Am I right?"

"Sure are," Doug said. "We overdo strength and endurance training while we teach the use of all the equipment and go over our procedures. By the time we get to the tower, they are ready to go."

"Do they believe that?"

Doug paused. "I think so."

"But you're not absolutely sure?" Phil asked.

Doug shrugged his shoulders. He looked at Phil and admitted, "Not a hundred percent sure."

Phil explained, "I used to make that same mistake selling products. I'd get to the end of explaining a product and ask for the order before I was absolutely positive they were ready to buy. I lost sales because of that."

Doug sat there, squeezing his chin in his hand, trying to figure this out. "So how can I be absolutely sure they believe they are ready?" he asked.

"Ask 'em!" Phil paused, smiled, and went on. "Ask 'em—long before they are being tested. First you need to compliment them on the effort they put in with the training. You set this up days in advance of your Tower of Power Day and I'll bet you get a different result."

Doug was buried in his notebook, so Phil waited until he looked up. "Remember—they need to build their confidence. It may take more than one session for you to build them up. Measure their attitudes. Pay attention. Start well in advance of the actual day. That's critical. Ask your most positive trainee something like, 'Look at your results. You are in the best shape of your life, aren't you? You feel your new power?' Then let the trainee gush about how improved they are."

Doug, slowly nodding his head, said, "Sure. And the next one will follow with positive comments too. I could imagine the trainees all growing in confidence. The positive vibe would make a huge difference."

"You really do get this, Doug. Makes me happy! But I've got more for you. Let me tell you about feel, felt, found."

Phil was looking forward to giving Doug another piece for his persuasion tool chest, so Phil jumped right in. "Early in my sales career, in a training class about overcoming objections, the trainer gave us a simple formula. I had no idea how powerful this concept was until I had used it—and hundreds of variations of it. Time after time it brought great success."

"Another sales trick?" Doug asked.

"Don't assume, or you might miss this. It's not some sales ploy. This pathway is a powerful and effective way of helping people who are having a tough time with anything. As we have agreed, persuasion is not exclusively tied to selling a product or service. Any time someone expresses difficulty with anything—this will provide a simple pathway to build a solution.

"So, there we were in a sales training class. The trainer said, 'When you hear an objection you can use this formula. All the objections we have been rehearsing would be perfect for this method. And when you hear an objection you have never heard or dealt with before, using this formula will buy you some time to think of an appropriate response. We call it Feel, Felt, Found. It is your way of escaping and overcoming someone's dilemma, situation, or objection. Write this down.'

"On a whiteboard, he wrote, 'I know how you feel. Lots of people have felt that way. What they have found is this.' Then he said, 'If they tell you they are too busy to meet with you. If they say they need to think about it. If they say they cannot afford it. For almost anything they say, you can respond by saying, I know how you feel. Lots of people have felt that way. What they have found is this…'

"One of the sales trainees asked, 'What do you say then, after you say, 'What they found is this,' then what do you say?'

"The instructor said, 'Try to think of a similar situation and tell them how you successfully dealt with it. There is no magic phrase. It's a process that will get them comfortable and allow you time to find a solution. You'll have to figure out what pathways to choose.' The instructor looked at the group, winked, and said, 'At least saying all that stuff, 'I know how you feel and lots of people have felt that way,' gives you precious time to think about what to say next.' The trainees all laughed.

"Here's how it actually works, Doug. The basics of this approach are simple. Three steps. Write these three phrases down.

"First one: I understand your situation. Second one: Your situation is familiar and something we've seen often before. Then the third one: Here is how we successfully dealt with it.

"Let me explain. 'Feel:' Your Feel statement shows understanding. It is a disarming technique set up to eliminate the possibility of confrontation. 'I know how you feel.' You have shown acceptance of their situation or circumstance. You are on their side. You agree. No conflict here.

"Next: 'Felt:' Felt is the part of the technique designed to appeal to the herd instinct. From what I've read, herd instinct is an inclination in people or animals to behave or think like the majority. In other words, people want to be part of a group. They find comfort and security in their group. So, if you can show them that others have had the same reaction to similar circumstances, it is comforting to them. With me so far?"

Doug kept writing, nodding as he took notes. "Last is 'Found:' This is where you offer solutions or plans to develop solutions. It's your pathway out of the dilemma. Here, let me give you a couple of examples:

"Feel: I can see you are upset. Felt: Anybody would be. Found: Here's how I can solve that for you.

"Here's another. Feel: Like anyone in a situation like this, you are obviously disappointed. Felt: It's a common reaction I've seen many times before. Found: The times we have had this happen before, here is how we successfully dealt with it."

Doug said, "Yeah—it's sinkin' in now."

"Great. Let me give you a couple more for insurance. Feel: I heard that news too. Felt: Lots of people are going to be affected by that. Found: Here's my plan to deal with it.

"And one more. Feel: I sympathize with you. Felt: I've seen tons of folks in the same spot. Found: You've got a couple of great choices here.

"Doug, play with this. Alter the formula and experiment. You've got a tremendous opportunity using feel, felt, found. You told me your beginning as a firefighter included that ten-story assault on the human body, didn't it?"

"Yep!"

"So, you really know exactly how they feel, don't you?"

"I do! I know how they feel!" Doug said. Phil could not only see Doug's glowing smile, Phil could hear his smile in his voice. Doug was getting it.

"What you were thinking back then, they all are thinking now. Tell them you know how they feel. Tell them you and every other trainee since the Tower was built, they all felt that same way. That's the 'felt,' now here's the 'found.' You told me the veteran firefighters were there, cheering you on. Tell them about the inspiration you and the other trainees found, and how that feeling of success and achievement gave you the courage that launched your career. That's using 'feel, felt, found.' Open a pathway for them where they see themselves succeeding. Can you do that?"

Doug was obviously inspired. He answered, "Sure can! And I can imagine the result. We can make the Tower of Power Day an exhilarating and fun event!"

The next Tower of Power Day, Doug was ready. He had done everything to prepare for an epic event, including inspiring his group. Every trainee believed they would make it to the top.

"Firefighters!" Chief Doug Ross bellowed into the megaphone, his voice echoing in the mountains. "Firefighters. I know how you feel. I even know what you're thinking. Some of you might even have doubts, though you are in the best physical shape of your lives. I was right where you are not long ago, and I felt the same way you do. That platform is so high up, it's hard to see. It looks like it touches the clouds. It doesn't. I found courage—you will too! We have a veteran stationed on every floor to encourage and cheer you on. The day I took on the tower, those cheers seemed to lift me to the top. They will lift you too. If you need help, we will be there for you. You will all make it to the top. You will dominate, and become powerful. That's why it is called 'Tower of Power Day.'"

Chief Ross continued, "The view from the top is awesome, and you'll be there feeling the exhilaration of conquering the tower. You will all become your own Tower of Power. We are Fire Rescue Master Station. We are the best!" Then Doug led a chant with the entire group. "Fire rescue master station, fire rescue master station, fire rescue master station." Each time it got louder. "Fire Rescue Master Station—let's GOOOOOO!"

They exploded onto the staircase. The voices echoed in the mountains. "Hurry! Hurry! Faster! Go, Go, Go!"

Though a couple trainees struggled right there at the end, with a little help from the veterans, they all reached the top. The congratulatory atmosphere made Doug know these were firefighters he could count on to be there on his team.

Doug said out loud, "Wow! Same tower. Same drill. Nothing changed but me. I changed—changed my perspective—changed my approach. Damn! No more Tower Challenge for us here at Master Station. It's Tower of Power from now on!"

Tips from the Communication Toolbox:

- *Promote the benefits, not the features.*
- *Give orders—get resistance; sell the 'why' of what you ask, and you will find continued compliance. Make the sale.*
- *Build people up so they have the confidence and power to act.*

CHAPTER 10

CHALLENGES

> Concepts:
>
> A philosopher from the 1900's said, "That which does not kill us makes us stronger." Life is filled with challenges. Overcoming them builds our character, especially the tough challenges. Working through them sharpens our minds. Getting it right builds our confidence. You are about to find ways of making your challenges more manageable—ways to make you stronger!

The Bonner breakfast room was packed—not for breakfast, but for an evening of celebration. It was Jason Bonner's retirement party. Guests were already seated but Phil and his wife, Kim, saw their name tags on a table near the front and grabbed their seats.

Phil whispered, "Hey Millie," as he realized she and her husband were sitting next to him. "Great to see you! You used to be the receptionist. Used to see you times I ate here."

She smiled. "I saw you too. Nina Ross was putting the guest list together and called me to see if I knew people from Jason's past who should be invited. I came up with a few. She was telling me about The Bonner and how great she was doing. Said you helped her a number of times. Well...surprise...surprise. You got on the guest list!"

Phil grinned, obviously proud. "I wondered how we got here. I'll have to thank her!"

Millie went on. "Us? We had to be here. I promised myself I would not lose touch with my co-worker friends. So many people leave a job and never see the people they spent so much of their lives with. Sad. I value friendships too much to just walk away. And Jason—he is like a brother to me." Millie saw Jason Bonner about to enter the room. "Oh look. It's Nina Ross. Jason Bonner is there behind her!"

Nina announced, "Welcome everyone! We are here tonight to celebrate!" As a magician would use a wave of their hand to reveal their surprise, Nina waved hers. "Mr. Jason Bonner!"

It was a standing ovation. As Phil glanced around the room, he saw his friends, Doug and Loretta Ross. In the beginning, Phil had trouble calling Dr. Ross by her first name. By now he felt totally comfortable calling her Loretta. Phil thought, *"I get a kick out of that pet name Doug has for her. Retti. But I would never call her Retti. When people fall in love, a pet name often follows. A pet name is private—personal. I'd never use the pet name that belongs to someone else."* At the same table with Doug and Loretta was a man Phil didn't recognize, but he saw Jaxie. She was standing there clapping next to the man. Phil thought, *"That guy must be her dad, Paul."*

The room quieted as guests took their seats. Jason beamed as he headed for the front of the room. Just then, Phil felt a tap on his shoulder. He turned to see a smiling face and extended hand. The man said, "Saw your name there." The man pointed at the card on the table. "Phil Stone, I'm Fred Freed. Doug Ross told me about you. You guys are good friends?"

"Yep—sure are!" an enthusiastic Phil said, "And I'd like to be yours!"

"Well come on and get yourself a real car—a Ford!" Fred said with a laugh and a big smile.

"Look." Phil pointed. "That guy over there—next to Jaxie Jackson. He's waving. Know him?"

Fred waved back, then looked at Phil and said, "That's her dad, Paul. I owe him a big one."

"Never met Paul. I kinda' know his daughter, though not real well. Jaxie and Nina Ross have been tight friends for ages." Phil looked at Fred. "So, you owe Paul a big one?" Phil asked.

"Yep. He saved my butt. It was a long ago Friday night. Our Grand Opening. We had hundreds of balloons. Streamers everywhere. We put a car up on a rotating pedestal with special lighting. It cost me an arm and a leg, but I wanted something impressive that would pique people's curiosity. I wanted them to be compelled to come into our showroom."

With a questioning look on his face, Phil asked, "Paul helped with that, did he?"

"Did he! I spent a fortune to advertise the event. It was my make-or-break night. If things didn't go perfectly, I stood to lose it all. I was banking on this—literally. I hit the circuit breakers to turn on the lights. Nothing. No power. The pedestal didn't rotate. The lights went dark. It was a disaster. Even my perimeter lights were flickering."

"Wow. Bet you were frantic. How did Paul solve it for you?" Phil asked.

"I was pacing around, trying everybody in the county, and no electrician replied. None! I left messages and emails, but it was Friday night. I couldn't think straight. Then this guy in a panel truck pulls in.

He says, 'You having electrical problems? Those lights aren't supposed to flicker and flash like that. Looks dangerous.' I didn't know what to say. Stunned, I guess. Then this guy said, 'I'm a journeyman. You know—an electrician. Want me to take a look?'"

"So, you must have a guardian angel? Me too!" Phil said.

"Never thought I had a guardian angel until that day. Thirty minutes later the lights stopped flickering, the platform started turning, and the spotlights glowed. People came swarming in. Paul hung around for well over an hour just in case something else went wrong. He saved us. And this will tell you something about Paul. When I asked him what I owed, he just said, 'You get me a sweet deal on my next car and I'm good.' That's all!"

"Oh, hey. Good stuff. Look. Jason is about to speak. Great to finally meet you!" Phil said as Fred turned and went back to his table.

Jason Bonner was a powerful speaker with a resounding voice. He must have thanked everybody in the room by name during his speech. As the evening went on, Phil had a chance to sit and talk with Jason. When the topic moved to The Bonner, Phil asked, "Your new manager—Delvecchio, right? Not here tonight?"

Jason shook his head. "Yeah. I know. Weird. He was invited. I'm a little disappointed."

"Me too. I was hoping to meet him." Phil replied. "It is a little weird."

"I spent months searching through candidates before I chose this guy. He seemed to have it all. His resume said, 'References available upon request.' So, I asked for some, and I even called them."

"You don't get much out of references, do you?" Phil asked.

Jason grinned. "I know. References are going to be biased. Who would be dumb enough to put down the name of someone who would give a poor recommendation? Smart candidates give themselves a guarantee. They get permission before putting someone's name down. Really sharp candidates even coach them with things to say—you know, things that would be pertinent to the job. If the job requires great attention to detail on spreadsheet work, and I hear the reference say, 'He's a great guy, and boy does he know his stuff when it comes to spreadsheets. He's a detail fanatic!' I know that candidate coached them. Tells me I've got someone who can make good things happen—someone who will find a way to get things done. That's the kind of response I got when I reached out to Delvecchio's references. Weak candidates give weak references."

"Funny!" Phil said as he stood there shaking his head. "You really know people, don't you? That's my passion too—figuring people out—learning what they think."

Jason let out a sigh. "Well, I hope I've figured this guy out, and Mr. Tony Delvecchio lives up to my expectations. Even though he was thoroughly vetted, I have this nagging doubt. Don't know why."

That night, as Phil drove away, Jason's words echoed in Phil's mind. Phil thought, "*I hope Delvecchio lives up to everybody's expectations too!*"

Three uneventful months went by at The Bonner. Nina felt strange having a new manager. Unlike the open-door policy that Jason Bonner lived by, she'd walk past Mr. Delvecchio's office, and the door was always closed. Even the Bonner staff seemed different—guarded and serious. The fun seemed to leave when Jason Bonner left.

It was late Friday afternoon, and Nina was anxious to get away from the hotel for the weekend. As she was about to leave, she looked down at the reception desk and saw a letter with her name on it. With intense curiosity, and a feeling of apprehension, Nina grabbed it and ripped it open. It started with, "Ms. Nina Ross. We regret to inform you…"

When her heartbeat stopped banging in her head, Nina called Jaxie. "Hey girl," Jaxie said as she picked up her phone. The caller ID showed it was Nina, but Jaxie heard nothing. "Nina? You there? Pocket dial? You there?"

"Can you hear me? Yeah. I'm here—kinda'."

Jaxie could feel tension in Nina's voice. "What's wrong? You okay? You sound stressed. You good?"

"No. I'm not good. I'm sitting in my car with a termination notice signed by that new guy, Tony Delvecchio. I'm shocked. But I'm okay. I've gone off the deep end too many times with a shocker like this. Not this time. Dad calls these our 'what now' moments. Helps me when I look at things that way. Just need to figure out my next adventure, I guess."

"What happened? You mess up?" Jaxie asked.

"No. This letter has a long, drawn-out explanation about an investment group taking over the property and going in another direction. I really don't understand."

"You get ahold of Jason Bonner yet?" Jaxie asked.

"No! What would I say?"

"Nina, this isn't one of those times when you use persuasion skills to learn what someone's thinking. This is point-blank time! You need answers!"

"Hmmm. You're right. Good idea. I'll ask Mr. Bonner. Knew you'd help. I'm on it!" Nina said, with power and conviction in her voice.

Jaxie said a quick, "Keep me posted," and hung up.

Nina knew this was much too important an issue to solve on the phone. To help her know what he was thinking, she needed to see Jason Bonner's facial expressions as she asked her questions. Nina drove to his home. Jason invited her in. They sat in the living room. Nina handed him her termination letter and watched his reaction.

"Nina, I'm embarrassed, and so incredibly sorry. I beg your forgiveness. I had no idea."

Incredulous, Nina asked, "How could something like this happen?"

Jason sat there wringing his hands, head slumped down, staring at the floor. He took a deep breath and continued. "Nina, can I tell you something and trust you to keep it to yourself? I don't want this to get out."

Nina sat back, curiosity growing, and calmly said, "Sure. I learned long ago to keep private conversations private. That's why people feel free to tell me things—private things. I don't share anything confidential—ever. So what happened?"

"I know that about you, and appreciate that. My mom is ill. Prognosis is not good. I thought I could take an early retirement and care for her while still keeping my interests in The Bonner alive. Somehow Delvecchio found out. He's a snake. That investment group he is part of is full of snakes! We took out loans to redo the breakfast room. Big dollars. Don't know how they did it, but his group bought up every one of The Bonner Hotel's loans and basically forced us out. By the time I realized what he was doing, it was too late. It was either take his offer to buy the place or fight him in court. I can't fight them—it could tie me up for ages. Gotta' take care of Mother." Still wringing his hands, he looked into Nina's eyes and said, "I had no idea. I'm so very sorry. It's just been a few months since I left, but I'm out of touch with Bonnerville. Don't know who's hiring. You got a plan? If I can help in any way…"

"I didn't realize your mom was sick."

Jason admitted, "Nobody did. I don't want the entire town to be telling me how to deal with this, or how sorry they are for me. So, I've kept it quiet."

"Don't worry about me, Mr. Bonner. I'll figure it out. You take care of your mom, okay?"

Jason nodded, gave Nina a fatherly hug, and led her to the door.

As she drove home, Nina put together her plan. She never had a resume, so that needed to be priority one. Then she'd blast it to everybody in Bonnerville who was hiring.

After spending hours creating an impressive resume, and sending it to almost twenty hiring managers right in Bonnerville, she waited. More hours passed—no return emails. None. Nothing.

The next morning, she expanded her search and sent her resume to another twenty in driving distance from Bonnerville. Again, she waited—and waited. Her eyes glazed over as she sat staring at her computer. Nothing!

Frustrated, she searched online for advice. Info told her how a cover letter helps candidates stand out. So, Nina composed a generic cover letter she could send with every resume, and resent it to everyone she had tried before. Again. Nothing.

Days of sending out resumes got no responses. Nina put the worry of not ever finding another job in the back of her mind. She decided to stop blasting the entire world and target specific jobs where her skills fit. She was well into planning when she checked her email and there it was—a response with the time and place for her first interview. She clapped her hands together and yelled, "Finally!"

Nina called Jaxie. When Jaxie picked up, she heard an excited squeal. "Yeeesss! I got one!"

"Awesome," Jaxie said. "What did ya' get?"

"My interview. I finally got one! I started thinking I may never find a job. Then I started freaking out about another 'what now' moment. I thought if I never found a job—I have no idea what to do next." Nina shook her fist and said, "But I'm gonna' make it happen!"

"Good for you, Nina. You deserve it. You've been stressin' way too much. So, what's the company? What's the job?"

As Nina opened her mouth to explain, a burst of fear swept over her. She thought, *"What if I go into all kinds of details, and it doesn't happen? What if I don't get the job?"* Nina said, "Listen. I'm afraid to jinx the whole thing. Love to tell you. Let me wait. Tell you after, okay?"

"Okay. I can deal with that," Jaxie replied. "So, when? You can tell me when, right?"

Nina smiled. "Tomorrow at ten o'clock. I'll call and fill you in."

That next morning Nina was up with the sun. She picked out her most corporate pantsuit, had a great breakfast, and was on her way out the door when an email hit her phone. It read, "Thank you for your interest in our company. We have selected and hired a candidate. We must cancel our meeting with you today. We wish you the very best in your quest for a new position."

Nina almost fell on the couch. She sat there, head in her hands, silently. She thought, *"Well, here I am! What now?"*

Nina pushed herself to believe. If she stopped believing she would find a great job, she would be willing a negative. No time for anything negative now. She'd experienced needing things in the past, and with over-the-top confidence, she was able to almost will things to happen. Staying positive was critical. Frustrated but determined, Nina kept looking—and looking. As she surfed through another recruiting website, she saw an ad for a Sales Assistant. "*Ah,*" she thought. "*I can do that. Sales—persuasion—that's me. I can do that.*"

Nina had become a successful Reservations Manager at The Bonner. She had never worked anywhere else. She was concerned. She needed to find a way to stand out with this application. She needed the hiring manager to take her seriously. But how? This ad was for a Sales Assistant. How could she show them a Reservations Manager would be the perfect fit for the Sales Assistant job? Then she had an idea.

Instead of heading the resume with the title *The Resume of Nina Ross* or *Nina Ross, Reservations Manager*, she thought of a great way to create a strong first impression. She thought, "*At the top of the resume, I'll put 'Nina Ross, Sales Assistant,' and then I'll add their company name. I'll start the resume and application with exactly what would be on my business card if I do get that job. That will catch their eye. Then I'll glorify my communication and persuasion skills in the body of the application. Can't wait to read more and see who this company is, and what they are all about. Hope it's perfect. I need it bad!*"

The ad excited her. All the details looked great. But when she got to the bottom of the ad, she gasped in amazement. It read, "Apply to Freedom Ford…attention…Fred Freed."

Tips from the Communication Toolbox

- *Let your guardian angel know you.*
- *Give of yourself and you will get back more than you give.*
- *True friendship is rare. Don't allow a great friend to drift away.*
- *Extensive research is no guarantee you've found the perfect direction to travel.*
- *There are times to employ persuasion techniques to discover someone's thoughts. Other times can require a point-blank question. Read the situation.*

- *Keep private conversations private. People will reveal themselves to you when they know you will honor confidentiality.*
- *Include a targeted cover letter with resumes. References need to approve their name on your resume, and coach them on what to say.*

CHAPTER 11

DEVELOPMENT

Concepts:

Being fired is embarrassing. It's deflating. It's an attitude and confidence killer. And it's also a clear signal for you to change course—move on. All things have an end—even those negative feelings you have will end. Find a niche where you can be a difference maker. Add value. When uncertainty accompanies opportunity, take a breath and rise to the occasion. Be a powerful communicator who never leaves people guessing.

Nina filled out the application and sent it in, but rather than waiting and hoping for a return call she might never get, she had a plan. She and Fred Freed met when Doug got her the Mustang a few years back. She'd seen him many times since. She had recently spent a few minutes chatting with him at Jason Bonner's retirement bash too. Her car wasn't even close to needing an oil change, but she scheduled an appointment anyway. She pulled into the busy service bay and walked inside to the service counter. There was Fred Freed! As Nina recovered from the luck of accidentally bumping into him, she said an energized, "Mr. Freed! Good morning!" He smiled back and gave a thumbs-up while he continued talking with his head mechanic. As he turned toward Nina, extending his hand, Nina said, "I want to thank you again for letting me store my car here for that whole summer years back. I meant to mention it last time we talked. I never did thank you personally. Just a 'thank you' card. It was the trip of a lifetime, and it wouldn't have happened without a safe place for my Mustang."

"Happy to help, Nina. And I remember getting that card. I appreciated that. One day I'll need something and I know you'd help me, right?"

"You bet, Mr. Freed. I'm ready to help you right now!" Aglow with enthusiasm, she said, "I just applied for your Sales Assistant position. Is it still open?" she asked, as she shook Fred Freed's hand.

"You did?" Fred asked, his head on a swivel, going back and forth. "We haven't found the right person yet. But I'm a little confused. Paul Jackson just ordered a new Ford for his Jaxie. She took her four-year plan and is graduating in only three years. Paul put the money he saved on a fourth year of college into a new Jaxie car as her reward. She told me you were working at The Bonner and how proud of you she is. You are thinking about leaving? You considering a career change?"

Nina didn't want to say out loud that she had been fired. She simply said, "Looks like The Bonner is going in another direction, so it's time."

"Really? Well okay then! Let's sit in the conference room and we'll talk," Fred said as he started walking down the hallway. "Follow me."

Fred kept smiling as he gestured for Nina to have a seat in the conference room. He sat at the head of the conference table and pointed to the seat next to him for Nina to sit down. "Figured we might as well be in here. This is where we run our weekly sales meetings, and the Sales Assistant sits right there where you are sitting now. The Sales Manager sits here where I'm sitting. So let me tell you about the job."

Nina pulled a notepad and her printed resume out of her bag. She was nervous, but Fred wasn't a stranger. She didn't know his true temperament yet, but the town thought highly of Fred Freed. With a deep breath, she was able to control her fears. She added a grin that told Fred she was comfortable, so he jumped in. "Sales Assistant works with the sales force helping, checking in paperwork, and sending out customer communications. Nothing too complicated. If you are ever here and the entire sales force is busy when a customer walks in, and it does happen, that customer is yours. You sell them a car and the commission is yours too. On sales meeting day—ours is every Tuesday—the morning starts in here."

Nina looked around the room. The conference table had twelve dark leather chairs. A dozen more were lined up at the back wall. Above them was a huge collage of pictures of the evolution of Freedom Ford. There was a much younger Fred with shovel in hand for the original ground-breaking right there in the center. On the side wall was a big video monitor and a glass write-on board. The other wall was floor-to-ceiling clear glass. It was an impressive place. She liked it.

"There's a strong salary, benefits, and paid vacations—all that," Fred paused, then enthusiastically added, "And remember—you get the commissions when you personally make a sale!"

They talked for close to an hour. He answered her every question. She answered his. It sounded perfect. Then Fred excused himself, saying he'd be just a minute. As Nina waited, her mind just kept spinning. Seconds seemed like minutes. She wanted this job. But what if she didn't get it? What could she do or say to lock up the Sales Assistant position?

What questions should she plan to ask when Fred came back? What should she do next?

She looked up and saw Fred reach for the handle on the glass door. She knew a look of fear and concern was showing on her face. That wouldn't do. So, she pressed herself to change it to a soothing smile.

As the door opened, Fred smiled back as he handed her a formal-looking document. He proudly said, "I had them print this offer letter. Let's go through it."

Nina got goosebumps when she realized that letter had her name printed on it. Salvation—it was a job offer! Then Fred said, "We'd love to have you here at Freedom!"

After getting her parents' blessing, she called Fred Freed and worked out the details of her starting at Freedom. She got off the call and let out a sigh of relief, thinking, *"Got that job! I persevered and did it! And, I'll never have to see that snake, Delvecchio, again!"*

Days passed. Nina was sitting in the family room, relaxing from a long week. "Nina. How do you like it there at Freedom?" Doug asked.

"So far it's just training. Sales meetings are exciting. Mr. Freed is great. He tells me I need to become a true expert in cars to make a difference. I want to be a difference-maker! There's a ton to know. But he's directed me to all kinds of resources, and I can do research beyond that. I feel good about it. He's given me a thirty-day target and, Dad, you'll love this. He made it one hundred percent clear how much I'd benefit by meeting the goal. He got me excited about reaching it."

"Fred's a sharp guy. He and Jason Bonner go way back—great friends. I like him too. Knew you would. What's your goal look like?" Doug asked.

"I need to know everything about Freedom Ford. He wants me to spend time with each employee so I know who can assist customers with what issues, and especially as I'm getting started, I'll know who can help me. We built a schedule together. And every day he wants to spend time cultivating customers. Sales stuff. How to figure out what people need, and then solve it for them with a Freedom Ford. He loved my understanding of questions. That felt solid."

Doug smiled. "I love that you get to sell there too. You're gonna' need to know about your competition too. Gotta' learn it all."

"I'm already digging into that, but it's on the next thirty-day plan."

"Proud of you, Nina. You'll do great at Freedom. Look what you accomplished at The Bonner. What stuff has Fred been teaching you?"

"Lots. But I really liked his idea about giving people a timeframe for everything."

"Timeframe?" Doug asked.

"Hot Potato, huh Dad?" Doug winked. Nina let out a sigh. "Okay, here you go, Dad. He told me I'd be fielding questions all the time. First, I need to find out specifically what the customer needs—just like I did at The Bonner. But if I get questions I can't answer, being so new, rather than leaving our customer on hold while I try to find help, which irritates people, I can simply ask if they would be kind enough to give me time to get the exact info they need. People like to be kind. If they say it's okay, I need to give them a timeframe. Rather than just telling them I'll call them back, I need to tell them when—when they can expect me to get back to them with that answer. It works both when a customer calls or stops in and asks a question. If I can run in the back and get them an answer, I need to give them an idea how long I will take. People need to know."

"That's a good one. Hate when I need help and they tell me they'll call back. They always take longer than I hope they will. But I do get pissed off when I call to get help and they say they are going to call back, but they never do. Timeframe. I like that!"

"Yeah. And sometimes the customer may be anxious, like you. I might think calling them back the next day is okay. They might be less patient than that. Mr. Freed had me picture being on the customer side, expecting a callback, and not getting it. They get more irritated by the minute until they finally explode and call us! Then we get a furious call, when we could have prevented it."

Doug nodded. "With a timeframe. Sure. You tell them you'll call back within the hour, and you've bought yourself that hour to get the info you need. If you know it's gonna' take more time, buy yourself more time, right?"

"You got it, Dad. But Mr. Freed added one more critical question," Nina said.

"What's that?"

"I have to make sure the customer agrees. I can say, 'I'll call you by the end of business today,' but I can't stop there. I have to add something like, 'That work for you?' and if they say it does, I'm golden—as long as I call them back when I've promised."

Doug was loving hearing his grown-up little girl becoming such a force. Nina went on. "Here's the cool part. If I don't get the info they need, I still must call them back on or before the time I promised."

"What do you tell 'em if you don't know anything yet?" Doug asked.

"The truth. I tell them I don't know yet, but I will soon, and I will solve things for them. Then I give them another time frame and ask if that works."

Doug smiled. "I like that." His smile transformed into a sly grin. "Hey, could you teach that time frame thing to your mom? Retti is always saying, 'Just a minute,' or 'I'll be right there,' and I never know if it's gonna' be a minute, or fifteen minutes. I try not to let it show, but that pisses me off sometimes too."

"Not me! I'm not gonna' try teaching Mom anything. She's tough!"

Doug thought for a moment and his eyes suddenly lit up. "How 'bout this? Next time you're at New Vision Optical, tell Mom you'd be happy to teach her receptionist about timeframes, and how important they are. Mom'll probably ask what it's all about. Then you can tell her, and sell her on it. Hey. If nothing else—it will help your mom's office."

"That's a sweet one, Dad. I can do that. But if she doesn't change her 'just a minute' thing, you need to take over. You are the best person on earth to sell Mom."

The following week Fred called Nina into his office. "We talked about the power of questions during your interview. I was impressed. I believe you'll impress the salespeople with some of your expertise in asking questions too. If you are up to it, I want you to cover the sales meetings for the next two weeks while our Sales Manager is away on vacation. Can do?"

Nina stood there, reeling, hoping to keep her composure, realizing she had little choice. "Sure!" she said, with as much confidence as she could project. She thought back to the persuasion and communication lessons she'd experienced. Though she'd only been at The Bonner for a few years, Nina had become a strong communicator. She smiled, thinking how grateful she was that she had taken the time to catalog those lessons. Now, with her extensive database at her fingertips, she was ready.

Tips from the Communication Toolbox

- *Be a difference maker—in everything you choose to do. Difference makers are the champions of forward progress.*
- *Always tell people what to expect. The only surprises allowable are positive ones.*
- *When challenged with a difficult task, rise to the occasion.*
- *Be persistent. Many things require more than one try.*
- *Whatever you do, become the expert. Don't short yourself.*
- *Take notes. Your notes chronicle the events of your life. Take clean notes. Save and use them.*

CHAPTER 12

MIND-READING TECHNIQUES

> Concepts:
>
> There are good questions, bad questions, and safe questions. Safe questions will bring you to their true thoughts. Questions are the answer. The person who asks the question is the person who controls the conversation. Ask yourself questions. Ask your team questions. Always ask questions—great ones. Here's how:

Nina found herself at the head of the conference room for the Tuesday sales meeting. A couple dozen salespeople were sitting there, poised. All eyes were on her, and here she was, running the show. Masking her jitters, she started with a quick welcome, and then she confided, "Look guys. I'm not here to teach you sales. This team is among the best in the country. Mr. Freed asked me to talk about questions." She looked at the group. Their fidgeting made her more nervous. She put power in her voice as she said, "How many of you are mind readers?" No response—just blank stares. A few were snickering. "I promise, I can show you how to read minds!" Then she boldly said, "Questions are the answer!"

She stayed silent, making direct eye contact with each one. Once she had their full attention, she said, "Today we are going to talk about questions—safe questions!" They all watched as she stood up. She stood tall and continued. "Picture this. You ask me, 'What's your favorite color?' If I say, 'I like green,' and you ask me, 'Why,' or 'What about green do you like?' I will not feel defensive. I know you are not judging me—you can't. My answer cannot be wrong."

Nina stopped and gazed over at the group. Two sitting in the chairs at the back were whispering to each other. "I plan on taking questions later, but until then, I'd appreciate your full attention." Again, she looked at the group, but this time she directed her gaze at the two whisperers.

She went on. "There are facts and there are opinions. In the day of Christopher Columbus, many scholars believed the earth was flat. Flat or round, there was no proof either way, so people were entitled to their opinions. They would discuss. They would debate. They might argue. But they could not be proven wrong. No one wants to be wrong.

"You ask, 'Do you like Bob Smith for State Senator?' and I say, 'No,' and you ask 'Why?' I could be proven wrong. I have to defend my position. Hard to persuade people who are being defensive. We'll take a dive into asking questions, and look at ways to open people up so they tell you what they are thinking." Nina looked over the group and asked, "We all good?" A couple thumbs up and some nodding heads built up Nina's confidence.

She continued. "If you liked that, you'll love this one." She wrote the words, 'interrogative tags' on the write-on board, looked back, and told them, "Any time you want the power of a question with only a statement in your mind, this technique works beautifully, and with any statement. Make the statement, and then add an interrogative tag, like 'isn't it, doesn't it, don't you, aren't you, won't we.' Make the statement into a question. The new car leather smells great, doesn't it? Chicken sounds good, doesn't it? I think you'd agree, don't you? We'll have fun, won't we? I'm satisfied, aren't you? The interrogative tag is easy, and works most every time, doesn't it? It will get you a better understanding of what the other person is thinking, won't it? We all should make a conscious habit of turning our statements into questions, using a little interrogative tag, shouldn't we? You get my point, don't you? But be careful. As you can probably tell, it can be overdone…can't it?"

The entire room burst with laughter. When the room calmed, Nina went on—on a roll. "This technique, using interrogative tags, is not just to sell cars. This is a powerful way to always tap into the thoughts of people—all people—anywhere."

Nina had their attention. She was having fun. Her anxiety had vanished. She explained further. "When you are asking questions there are methods that will not put the customer on the defensive. A question like, 'Tell me why you are not buying this car?' makes our customer feel they have to justify themselves. As they verbally defend themselves, they grow more immovable. As they state their position for the world to hear, their words echo in their mind, moving them further away from where you want their mind to be. That's not good. Asking them for specific information they may not easily answer can create fear. What if you ask their opinion? An opinion can have an opposing side, an opposing position. Someone could challenge that opinion as being incorrect. They could be wrong. If they are afraid to be wrong, they will close down, not open up. That's what questions are supposed to do—open people up so you can know what they are thinking—so you can help them. If the question makes them uncomfortable, it's the wrong question.

"You never want to ask a question that might intimidate. You want people to feel free to be honest. Ask them a question where they cannot be challenged for being wrong. That is always the best direction to travel. Some of the safest questions will ask about feelings. If I ask you how you feel about anything, your answer, whatever it may be, cannot be wrong. It's your feelings!"

Nina wrote the word 'Feelings' on the write-on board, surveyed the room, and went on. "Bet I know what you guys are thinking." She smiled. "You're thinking you could ask people how they feel in a car you're hoping they will buy." A bunch of them nodded. "You can ask anybody how they feel about anything. It's a universal truth. However, they feel, they're right!" Nina went back to the write-on board and wrote the words: 'How do you feel about,' and she drew a line after that sentence, turned to the group and said, "Let's fill in the blank. Let's make a list. How do you feel about…?"

Members of the group fired off a bunch of examples. "Freedom Ford? About convertible tops? About our five-star builder program? About seeing this car in your garage? About our service pledge?" They kept going.

Nina took control. "Perfect, but don't stop there," she said. "How do you feel about chocolate? How do you feel about beards? How do you feel about helping me? How do you feel about anything—it works." The salespeople were smiling and shaking their heads—some with more thumbs up. "But just like those interrogative tags," she warned. "You can overdo it in one conversation. It's a tool I keep in my communication and persuasion toolbox. Here's another one that tends not to intimidate. Get people to rate things."

On the write-on board, Nina wrote the words 'One to Ten.' "Asking people to rate things is safe. Their rating cannot be wrong. It's their judgment, and who could challenge that? That's partially why people love to rate things. The judge gets the power. Everybody enjoys power, so people are incentivized to be the judge."

By raising her hand, Nina signaled to her audience she wanted them to raise their hands if they agreed with what she said. She then asked, "You guys ever 'like' a post or picture you find online?"

Every hand went up. Nina nodded and went on. "People give 'likes' and 'thumbs up' in social media and texts all the time. They are also willing to rate things on a scale of one to ten. It's safe. Let me explain. In an anonymous opinion poll, answers cannot be challenged, so people take surveys and answer opinion polls freely. If no one knows who filled out the survey, no one can challenge what they say. When you see reporters asking regular folks their opinion—what they think of the issues of the day, many people decline to answer. They know once their opinion is out there for all to see and possibly criticize, they risk being called 'a fool.' They are afraid of being publicly challenged. When given the chance, people may feel safe enough to give their opinion, but better yet, get them to rate things on a one to ten scale. Why? Rating things is subjective. Whatever answer they give cannot be wrong. It is their opinion—but without the possibility of an opposing side. If they rate something as a five or an eight, who could challenge their rating? It is so much easier to answer questions with no chance of being wrong. See what I mean? Ask them safe questions where their answers can't be challenged, and they will give you the information you need to create that win-win. You will know what they are thinking!"

The salesperson closest to Nina was amazed. She said, "Wow. I never realized how powerful rating one to ten can be!" Just then Fred Freed walked into the sales meeting, snuck to the back and sat at the back wall, listening.

"It gets even better," Nina said, as she smiled and winked at Fred. "There are more benefits waiting for you when you ask people to rate how you personally performed. You ask, 'On a scale of one to ten, ten being the best, how would you say I have taken care of you today?' Chances are they will rate your performance a bit higher than they truly believe because they don't want to disappoint and hurt your feelings. If they would have told a friend the experience was good and would have rated you at a six, they may tell you directly to your face you got an eight or a nine. The benefit to you? Just by them saying that higher rating they will remember the experience in a more favorable light. By voicing the higher number, they start to sell themselves on a higher perceived value of your proposition, making it easier for you to move them up to the ten. It is a lot easier moving someone from an eight to a ten than from a six to a ten.

"Imagine when you are showing a car to a prospective customer, you ask, 'On a scale of one to ten, ten being the best, how excited are you about driving this car?' If you get less than a ten, you know you have more work to do before you can hope to close the sale."

"Here's another one. 'On a scale of one to ten, ten being the best, how clear a picture did I paint for you about our warranty?' See how much better a question that is than asking what they think about, or if they like the warranty?

"You guys like it, rating one to ten?" Nina asked with a big grin. "Do you see the power?"

The entire team was nodding and making comments. It started getting loud, so Nina raised her voice and continued. "And you can use this with people anywhere, all the time. You go to a movie with a friend—maybe a restaurant—or to a new store, and you want to know what they thought about it. Ask them, 'On a scale of one to ten, ten being the best, how did you like it?' and then watch and listen. They'll tell you more. Remember, discovering what people are thinking is the most valuable information in your quest to help those people." Nina paused and graciously said, "Thanks you guys. You made my first solo sales meeting work. Hope it helped! Now go give your customers some Freedom!"

They gave Nina energized and sincere applause. As everyone filed out, Nina stood in the doorway. Many of them gave a positive comment and a handshake. Nina felt exhilarated—filled with pride. Alone now in the conference room, she plopped down in the chair at the head of the table, slumped back, and took a huge breath. "*I did it,*" she thought. "*Seemed like they liked the stuff I covered too.*"

Fred Freed returned to the room and shut the conference room door behind him as he said, "That was great, Nina. I even learned a few things."

He sat in the chair across from her as she admitted, "I was scared at first."

"First time I had to do a sales meeting, I was scared too. I wanted to get in here with you this morning, but a pressing call came in. I had to take it. By the time I got in here, you were in total control. It was obvious. You had the whole team right there in the palm of your hand. Out in the hall, a bunch of them told me they were very impressed!"

"Thanks, Mr. Freed. I live to provide value. I'll be ready for the next meeting too. I've learned a ton in the last three years since high school. But you! You've been in the car business your entire career. You've already given me some great coaching. I know there's more coming too. It's exciting!"

Fred smiled and said, "Indeed, I have learned a lot in the car business. But cars were not my first business venture. I made my first fortune in bottles." Fred chuckled as he handed Nina a bottle of cold water. "Not these plastic bottles. Glass. Here, have some water. Take a break, and I'll tell you how it happened."

Nina smiled, cracked open the water bottle, took a sip, and said, "Love to hear it."

"My parents bought their first house just outside of Bonnerville in 1956," Fred began. "Mom always shopped at the A&P for groceries. Sometimes I'd go with her to help. Mom handed me a six-pack of empty soda bottles and asked, 'See that counter over there? Give these bottles to that man and he will give you money for them.'

"Mom was well into filling her cart when I found her in the aisles. 'Here you go,' I said as I dropped two nickels and two pennies into her hand. 'Why do they pay for worthless old bottles?' I asked.

"Mom told me, 'They do special things to make those bottles like new and they use them again. They call it recycling. You can keep the change,' she said.

"I suddenly had money I could spend as I pleased! Though all the cash in my piggy bank was actually my money, Mom would not let me spend it without permission. I never came up with a good enough reason to take money out of my piggy bank. Little Fred was not skilled enough to sell Mom. I remember picking up that piggy bank to see how heavy it was. I'd shake it to hear the coins clang inside. My mouth would water as I'd picture taking that money and buying bags of candy. It was quite a temptation. But then it got even worse.

"Mom decided to teach me the value of saving my money. But this experience taught me the importance of listening—really listening. She took me to United Bank and we opened an account with the entire contents of my piggy bank. There was every penny, nickel, dime, quarter, and paper dollar I had—all of it there on the counter. After every cent I had in the world was in the teller's drawer, she smiled and handed me a skinny little three-by-five-inch book. 'Here is your passbook. Your money is all right in here,' she said.

"I stared at that little book. Was this a real magic trick? On TV magicians pull huge white rabbits out of empty hats. I loved magic tricks. I was excited. What magic could the teller have used to get all my money into this little book? The moment we got outside I hurriedly opened the book. No money! My cash was gone!

"Mom tried to comfort me. 'Fred—it's okay. Your money is in the bank. See—right here.' She pointed to where the teller had just stamped my bank balance amount. 'You have twenty-eight dollars and twelve cents. The bank is saving it for you. It is still yours. They pay you to keep your money in their bank. And we can take some or all of your money back out of the bank any time you want, okay?'

"Sniffling, I said, 'Okay. I can take it back out when I want?' Mom nodded. 'Can I have it now?'

"Mom sternly said, 'Now Fred. Don't worry. Let's save even more, and one day you will have a lot of money. Save it for a rainy day when you need it.'

"Days later I woke to the sound of thunder. I jumped out of bed and ran to the window, threw open the curtains, and watched the sky flash with lightning bursts as rain poured from the sky. 'It's here—my rainy day. I gotta' get Mom!'

Nina, recognizing the absurdity of Fred's thoughts, tried to stifle a laugh. It turned into a giggle she had a tough time controlling.

Fred smiled at her and went on. "Jumping up and down with enthusiasm, I told Mom it was time. It was a rainy day. 'No Fred,' Mom explained, shaking her head. 'Save it for a rainy day' is an expression. Your money needs to stay in the bank.'

"As I turned around to go sulk in my bedroom, all I said was, 'Oh.' Mom told me I could have my money on a rainy day. Then Mom said, 'No,' 'save it for a rainy day' was an expression. Mom said, 'When hell freezes over' is an expression too.' Hell doesn't freeze over either. Obviously, I was missing something—this all didn't make sense.

"I learned to pay close attention to the words people used. I could hear something and completely miss the point. Listening closely proved critical to understanding what the person meant by the words they chose. I understood the importance of examining the unsaid words there between the lines too—the unsaid is often invaluable. If I wasn't one hundred percent sure what people meant, I learned to formulate questions and probe until I was sure I understood. Great lesson. Questions are the answer.

"Well, this bottle thing was not an expression. I gave the man old bottles. He gave me money. Next to the A&P was Walgreens where I could get a pack of Topps baseball cards with a big chunk of Bazooka Bubble Gum in it—all for a nickel. I bought two packs and a handful of penny candy with the pennies.

"Later that week I set out on my bike to search for treasure. I knew I could find bottles, and I was right. There were dozens on the side of the road. The problem? That basket on my bike only held a few bottles. I had to make multiple trips to get them home, and couldn't get a big load to the A&P. My solution? I begged Santa to get me a Radio Flyer wagon!

"Christmas morning, there was my wagon under the Christmas tree. I was in business! I'd put a couple dozen cleaned bottles in my Radio Flyer wagon and set off for the mile-long walk to the A&P. Less than a half hour later I'd be on the return trip home with ten packs of baseball cards to sift through while chomping on more bubblegum than could actually fit in my mouth.

"You know what that taught me, Nina?"

Nina grinned. "Hopefully you learned not to bite off more than you can chew!"

Fred laughed. "That's a good one! But really, it taught me the importance of having the proper tools to get any job done. Through the years I've seen so many people start something and scrimp on the tools that will prove critical to their success. You need a website? Get one. Rent a location. Design a sign. Get the tools you need to make the project work. You've heard people say, 'Dress for success.' Dress to fit the role you play. You want to attract people to you? You need to be impressive. The wagon was a tool that made a critical difference for me. Without that wagon, I would never have inspired my friends to work with me. I was the guy with the tool. It got my bottles to the store, and it impressed all my friends. That wagon helped me persuade all my friends to share in the profits. Gotta' have the right tools. Make sense, Nina?"

"The right tools—makes sense," she said. "Mr. Bonner was a great coach. My dad and my dad's friend, Phil—they've been coaching me too. Phil talks about tools. But his tools are mostly words. He's helping me build my persuasion toolbox!"

"Good point, Nina. Tools are not always tangible. I remember Phil. Met Phil Stone at Jason's retirement party. Good guy?"

Nina said, "Yep. You're right! He was there too. Good guy. And I'd bet he would have loved your bottle story. It has sales and persuasion all through it. So, your friends got in on the action too? How'd that happen?"

"Well, on one side of our house, my dad parked his car. The other side was just gravel and the perfect hose spigot lived there. I hosed off bottles while dreaming about getting another Mickey Mantle or Roger Maris baseball card with my next haul."

"Who?" Nina asked.

"Funny," Fred said. "Those are stars from before your time. Each generation has their stars. I wonder who yours will be. As a young boy, my stars, like Mantle and Maris, were on the cover of those baseball cards. My friends were all starting baseball card collections. Mine dwarfed every one of theirs. I had so many, I could trade five cards of mine for just one card of theirs if I needed it to complete my collection. I never confided in anyone how I got dirty bottles and turned them into my baseball card dynasty. If they knew, they would go out and find their own bottles, leaving less for me to harvest.

"One day Perry Barks caught me rolling a load to the A&P. 'Where are you going?' he demanded, as if I reported to him.

"Surprised, I blurted out my secret. 'I'm going to the A&P to cash in these bottles. That's how I get the money for all my baseball cards. This shiny red wagon was from Santa. He got it for me so I could get more bottles to the store. My bike basket is way too small,' I admitted.

"Perry shook his head as he said, 'Gosh, I wish I had a wagon.'

"I was thinking, *'Boy am I glad you don't!'*

"Then it hit me: none of the kids in the neighborhood had a wagon but me! 'Perry, how 'bout this?' I asked. 'What if you found some bottles and brought them to my house? I could clean them up and use my wagon to take them to the A&P. You wouldn't have to do anything but find them. I will do the rest. And I will do all that work and be willing to split what I get with you. Each bottle gets us two cents. I will split that with you fifty-fifty. I will give you a penny a bottle. What do you think?'

"It was less than fifteen minutes and there was Perry with four bottles, one was a quart size. 'What about this big one?' he asked. In the print on the label, it said there was a five-cent refund. 'I'll double you on those. Two cents.' He handed me the four bottles and then stuck out his hand. I hadn't given any thought to paying him before I cashed in his bottles, but the look on his face told me if I wanted him to do this anymore, I needed to go up to my secret place where I stashed my bottle money and get him five cents. Nina, you gotta' pay close attention to facial expressions.

"I dropped a nickel into Perry's hand. He said, 'Thanks Fred. Hey, Ricky asked me what I was doing and I told him, and he wants to get bottles too. I told him to talk with you, okay?'

"Every day I had more bottles to clean up and cash in. My friends had more baseball cards than they knew what to do with too. Why? Instead of keeping my secret to myself, I learned the power of 'team.' I could never have become the 'bottle baron' with only my efforts. And all my friends made more money than they could have made alone. And, we had fun! Working together—much better than working alone. As a team, we all scored. I've thought about my bottle business many times over the years. It was fun while it lasted, but everything comes to an end."

Nina was smiling as she said, "Great story, Mr. Freed. Lots of gems in there. You were born to be running your own show, and you were lucky. Some people never figure out the importance of a team approach. You were young when you found the benefits!"

Fred smiled.

Tips from the Communication Toolbox

- *Ask questions that do not intimidate so people answer freely.*
- *Safe questions where the answer cannot be criticized are the best choice.*
- *There are life lessons in both positive and negative experiences. Seek the lessons. Find them. Then use what you learn to improve the quality of your choices you make in the future.*
- *Determine what tools are needed to excel in every endeavor—and get them. Don't scrimp.*
- *When it comes to decisions, two heads are better than one. Better than that—use the entire team!*

CHAPTER 13

ELEVATION

Concepts:

With every problem comes opportunity. The bigger the problem, the greater that opportunity. If it's a personal problem, aside from the benefit of eliminating your own issue, you gain knowledge—experience. When you inadvertently create the problem, you have to do more than just solve it. You must go overboard with your solution. Go well above, and far beyond. Blow them away with your efforts to solve things. Keep your eyes open to see the positives. All problems come with opportunity.

It was always a special day when Nina had a customer come in and drive off in their brand-new car. Some customers picked a car from inventory, right there on the car lot. They might buy a car and drive away in it that same day. But Derek Jones ordered a custom version. He waited weeks. Nina helped him customize his car with special candy apple red paint, a sports package, the ultimate sound system, and that tan convertible top.

Derek had lots of cars over the years, from clunkers to fine rides, but never one with that real new-car smell. He was so excited when he received a call confirming that the car was on the lot. His Uber driver dropped him on the doorstep of Freedom Ford. There was Nina Ross, his salesperson, smiling and waving him over.

"Hey, Derek. Welcome. Are you excited? Let me escort you to your brand-new ride. It's this way," she said.

He couldn't wait to see it. Derek had pictured himself behind that wheel, wind in his hair, stereo blasting, sailing down that highway, without a care in the world. There it was, right there in front of him.

"What?" Derek yelled. "The top is wrong. It's black!" He looked at Nina. She could see the pain in his face as he asked, "What happened?"

Nina was stunned. "Oh Derek. I'm so sorry. I don't know how this could have happened, but we will make it right."

"How?" Derek asked, with both sorrow and irritation oozing from his being.

"Wait here. I'll be right back," she said. Nina had never seen anything like this at Freedom Ford. She was shocked, and way out of her comfort zone. She couldn't believe she had missed the top color when she checked his car. Now she had a big problem to work through. Smart of her to escape to re-compose herself. She decided to bring in the big guns. Having someone of higher authority join Derek and Nina sends a message to Derek that he is important. A higher-up may be able to offer solutions that Nina could not. On this one, she needed as much help as possible.

Derek stood silently, staring at his imperfect new car when Nina brought help. An older man dressed in suit and tie, reached out his hand and said, "I'm Mr. Freed. We apologize for this mistake, but we have a plan."

"You're Mr. Freed? Aren't you the owner of Freedom Ford?" The relief Derek felt being introduced to the owner was obvious, both in his tone of voice and his facial expression. Watching his demeanor change, Nina took a breath and relaxed as Fred took over.

"That's me," Mr. Freed said. "So, here's the plan. We offer loaner cars to our best customers when they need service. We just completed the inspections on a car we took in trade last week."

Derek pictured some old clunker he would be offered instead of driving off in his candy apple red convertible with that soft tan top.

"We normally don't lend a car like this, but in your case, I will get it done. You deserve it." As Derek's mind raced, wondering where this was going, an awesome blue convertible Jaguar pulled up in front of them. "Let's fill out some paperwork for insurance purposes. They tell me we will have your black top replaced with the tan one you ordered in two weeks. Until then, you are welcome to borrow this. That help?" Mr. Freed asked, as he extended his hand to shake Derek's.

With a smile that lit his entire being, Derek aggressively shook Mr. Freed's hand—and Nina's too. A few minutes later Derek drove off the lot in a car he had only dreamed of riding in, let alone driving for a couple weeks. He was thrilled!

Two weeks passed. Derek's car was ready as promised, a trademark of Freedom Ford. They delivered on promises. Derek turned in the Jag and put down that tan top on his new car as he drove off the lot.

It was a month later. "Nina Ross to Mr. Freed's office please," came over the intercom.

Nina walked into Mr. Freed's office. She had printed a new five-star review from the company's Google account. "Look at this," she said, as she handed the one-page document to him.

Mr. Freed had a document in his hand too. "Look at this!" he said. It was a full-page glowing testimonial from Derek that had come in the day's mail. "And he put it up on Google too? Major score, Nina!"

HOW TO NOT LOSE FRIENDS AND FIGHT WITH OTHER PEOPLE

Nina said, "I've worked here at Freedom long enough to see trends. We've taken care of lots of customers here since I started. I've seen great one-liner reviews, but never anything like this!"

"Nina Ross, line one please," came over the intercom.

"Take it here, Nina," Mr. Freed told her, as he pointed to his desk phone.

"This is Nina Ross. How may I help you?" she asked.

"Hi Nina. My name is Wayne. I work with Derek Jones. He said you took great care of him, and I need a car. When can I come in to see you?" Nina set the appointment, grinning at Mr. Freed.

Then Mr. Freed said, "In all the years I've been in the car business, I've seen this same thing happen dozens of times. That is why I went so far out of our way to solve Derek's issue. Our customers expect to get exactly what they bought. We give it to them, and they are satisfied. No big deal—nothing special. Nina, have you ever gone to a fine dining restaurant and gotten good service?"

"Sure. We went out to The Angelica for Italian last weekend. I had a double-date with my girl, Jaxie."

"And did you get what you expected? Was the experience what you had pictured?"

"Yeah. We had reservations. Our table was great. Service was good and the food is always great there," Nina replied.

"So, you got what you expected. And I'll bet you didn't put up some flowery review online, did you?" Mr. Freed asked.

"Uh, no. You're right."

Then Mr. Freed asked, "Now, have you ever gone out to a restaurant and had something go wrong, like something is way over or undercooked? Then you call your server, and they get it fixed in a heartbeat, and when you get the bill, you realize the restaurant gave you your meal for free to make up for their error?"

"I get it," she said. "I've had that happen a couple times, and each time I've been shocked at how they bent over backwards to fix my food. And, yes, I have told all kinds of people about how great they were."

Mr. Freed nodded and said, "Our customers may give us a thumbs up or even a good review, but nothing like what Derek Jones did here in his testimonial. He gushed with praise—an entire page full of accolades. He praised the entire Freedom Ford team, and mentioned you by name. Now you can show customers that testimonial. It's a great credibility builder you have now. Here's why he gushed so much: When there is a problem, and the worse the problem, the more important this is—we need to go overboard in our efforts to fix things. When things go wrong, customers picture the worst possible outcome. Maybe they have had tough times resolving things in their past. Why they dwell on the negative, I don't know, but they do. And while they are going down that negative rabbit hole, if we catch them and pull them back up with an over-the-top positive experience, they are blown away."

Nina sat down, pulling her chair closer to Mr. Freed's desk. She wanted to take in every word. "The lesson," he said, "is this: When customers get what they expect—nothing more, nothing less, don't wait for them to tell the world. If you ask them, they'll be positive—so ask. But you cannot expect them to do or say much about the experience without your prompting them. When they get less than they are owed, they get vocal. These negatives can kill. That's why it is so important to cultivate communication skills—to handle those rare, but tough situations. On the other hand, when customers get more than they ever imagined, they feel blessed. They feel special. You made them feel special, and they will never forget how great that felt. They want to share their joy, and they tell people. Never miss the opportunity to transform a negative situation into a stellar event."

"Love it," Nina said. "I'm going to carry that with me. Mr. Freed? Please don't hesitate to offer me more of these nuggets."

Days went by. Nina's events calendar showed it was the day she would meet with Wayne Simonton. She was excited. Since he was a referral from Derek, who was blown away by the Freedom Ford experience, she anticipated an automatic car sale, bringing her to the top of the sales board—amazing for the Sales Assistant. A voice came over the intercom. "Nina Ross to the showroom floor. A customer is waiting."

As Nina rushed into the showroom, she got a glimpse of Wayne. He looked so familiar. No matter how hard she tried, she couldn't place him. He was a tall, distinguished looking man, impeccably dressed in suit and tie, and he carried himself like a winner. The dark wavy hair, greying at the temples, was a look she remembered, but she had no idea from where or when. She extended her hand as she said, "Welcome to Freedom Ford, Mr. Wayne Simonton. I'm Nina Ross. Thanks so much for coming in."

He smiled. As he shook her hand, he said, "Make you a deal. If I can call you Nina, you can call me Wayne."

"It's a deal, Wayne. My pleasure to meet you. And when you called you said you work with Derek Jones?" she asked.

"Derek works in the IT department at Allworld Insurance."

"Oh. That's right. I remember him telling me that. So, you're at Allworld?"

Nina gestured toward her glassed-in cubicle where she had a small desk and two side chairs for guests. Wayne sat as Nina rounded her desk. As she sat down, he said, "You don't remember me, do you?"

"You're right, and it's driving me nuts. You look so familiar. I know I've bumped into you before, but I can't for the life of me dial in how or when."

"Remember the summer outing Allworld runs every year at The Bonner?"

Nina snapped her fingers and said, "Aha! That's it. You were at the Allworld Picnic on the grounds behind The Bonner. I must have seen you there. I actually planned one of those events with a high-up manager at Allworld. I think her name was Sarah. You know Sarah?"

"Yep. She's my direct assistant."

"Your assistant?" Nina asked, shocked that the lady who ran the entire event for Allworld could work for Wayne. Before he could answer, Nina continued. "Ah. Now I remember. You were in a t-shirt and shorts, right?" Wayne nodded. "And I saw you there talking with Sarah. You didn't come off like an authority figure. You seemed like just one of the team. I remember now."

"I'm the General Manager at this Allworld branch. I run the place," Wayne said proudly. "I like to delegate. I don't walk around like I'm top dog or something. I try to lift up all the members of the team. Responsibility empowers them. We outline a task together. Then they grab the ball and run with it. I help where needed, and always give away any credit."

"I'm impressed," Nina said. "I've had two bosses, and both operate like that. They are special. I love them both. Jason Bonner was the first. When he retired, I found myself here at Freedom with Mr. Freed." Nina took a breath and said, "Well, now that you've blown me away, what can I do for you?"

"I came in to order one of those big SUV's that have a third-row seat. Need to tote team members to events. But I have another motive."

"Another motive?" Nina asked.

"I saw you in action at that summer picnic. When I told Jason how impressed I was, he couldn't stop glorifying you and what you had accomplished at The Bonner. Then he told me your dad is Fire Chief, and your mom runs New Vision Optical. Never met your dad, but these glasses look familiar?" Wayne reached up and took his dark rimmed glasses off so Nina could read the insignia on the inside of the temple. In small white lettering it said, "New Vision Optical."

"Ha. Those are Mom's glasses!" Nina exclaimed.

"Yep. I've been going to see Dr. Ross for years. That next time I stopped in, I told your mom how impressed I was with her daughter running the entire show for us at the summer picnic. She told me you had joined Freedom Ford. That same day Derek pulls into the parking lot in this awesome Jag. Blew me away. Then he tells me how Nina Ross made it happen. Everywhere I turned—Nina Ross, Nina Ross, Nina Ross. I had to meet you."

Blushing, Nina said, "Gosh. Small world, isn't it?"

"And the bigger your personality, the smaller that world gets!" Wayne announced, those words echoing in Nina's mind. "Before we take care of my new car, let me ask, what do you like most about Freedom Ford?"

Without hesitation she said, "The people. The team here is awesome. Everybody pulls together. Love that. And I enjoy helping customers." Nina paused. "It's not all fun and games. We solve problems. Sometimes tough ones."

"Like Derek getting the wrong car," Wayne said, as he gave a wink. "But you came off like a champion on that one." Nina nodded and smiled. "Anything you don't like here—something that could be better?"

"No. It's all good," Nina said, thinking about what to admit to someone she had just met. "The hours every weekend are tough. Pay is great, but I get a good chunk of my pay in commission, and some weeks it's up and some it's down. But those are little things. All good."

"It would probably be close to perfect if you worked Monday through Friday with almost every weekend off, and had a consistent paycheck week after week, wouldn't it?"

"More than close—it would be perfect!" Nina proclaimed.

"May I borrow that pen?" Wayne asked, as he pointed to Nina's cup of pens there on her desk. She handed him a pen, wondering why he wanted it. She had yet to start the paperwork for his car purchase. She watched as he scribbled something, then slid the paper he'd been writing on over to her. There was a number written on it. A big number. She could feel something major was happening. Chills ran down her spine as he said, "What if you made this, plus a bonus, and no weekends? We want you at Allworld!" Nina sat back in her chair, speechless. "I ran the idea by the Allworld team, and it was unanimous. I know this came at you out of nowhere. Fred's got a good crew here at Freedom. I know he thinks the world of you. A guy like Fred would never hold you back." He smiled and added, "And it's not like you'd be moving to New York or somewhere. You'll still be here in Bonnerville."

Nina sat there, stunned. She thought, *Maybe this is time. Maybe this is meant to be. That salary is almost twice what I've been making. I learned so much from Mr. Bonner. Then Mr. Freed took it up another notch. Maybe I'm supposed to do this."*

"I'll need to give notice," she said, as if asking permission. She had gotten completely carried away with the entire idea. Then a question popped into her mind. "At Allworld—what do you see me doing? What would I be?"

"Account Manager," Wayne said. "Picture this," he said, looking up as if he saw her imaginary office in the clouds. "You'll have a personal assistant right outside your door. Your office will be spacious." Wayne smiled as he waved his hand, highlighting how small her Freedom office was. "The sign on the door says, 'Nina Ross, Account Manager.' Like the look of that? How's it sound?"

Her grin made it hard to speak. She only was able to say, "Sounds great!"

She gave her notice, and the two weeks flew by. Fred Freed had a strained frown as Nina walked into his office. He powered into a smile as she sat down. "As much as it pains me to say it, we want to congratulate you on your new position at Allworld Insurance. We just hate to see you go, but I know this is an important step for you and your career."

Nina fought away tears. She had fallen in love with Freedom Ford. She knew all things end, and all endings come with some pain. She sat in the chair in front of Fred's desk and tried to keep her mind on her future.

"Nina," Mr. Freed said. "I am impressed with your growth. You are a great student. Every time I give you a nugget, you study and practice until it truly becomes yours. You are destined for great things. Let me tell you a quick story. A thousand years ago, a game called 'the carosella' was born. Soldiers would ride in circles on horseback and challenge each other, testing their skills. Years later the French tamed the game by placing highly decorated wooden horses on a circular platform. Servants would rotate the circular platform while the noble children, dressed in their finery, would ride the horses of 'le carrousel.' Games were created for the riders too. In one version, the riders would try to spear a brass ring. The brass ring became a treasured and sought-after prize.

"Motors replaced the man-powered versions in the 1900's and carousels often had a mechanical arm just out of reach of the carousel riders. On the end of that arm was…a brass ring. If a rider was brave enough to lean out, their butts hanging off the horse seat, and grab a brass ring, it was their prize and they could keep it. Another ring would pop up in its place for the next rider's joy.

"Going after the brass ring became a metaphor for going after a goal. Actually winning the brass ring meant achieving great success!

"Nina, I have been honing and tweaking the techniques I've been teaching you for over forty years. I have had the pleasure and the honor of teaching these approaches to hundreds of aspiring salespeople. I have seen lives changed. Don't let this go to your head, but in all those years, I have never found someone as fired up to learn as you. I see you thriving at Allworld. If you can find the power to keep moving forward, this world is your carousel, and I know that your brass ring is out there, just waiting for you to seize it. Let's make sure, whatever life has in store for you, that we keep in touch, okay? One day when the brass ring is in your hands, come see me…and bring your brass ring with you. I can't wait to see it!"

Tips from the Communication Toolbox

- *When faced with a tough issue, bring in the big guns. Get help from someone in a higher station to show sincerity.*
- *Deliver on promises.*
- *Provide more than people expect. Wow them.*
- *Life is a mysterious journey. Keep your eyes open. Ask questions. Pay attention.*

EPILOGUE

THE ACCIDENT

It was Friday at about four in the afternoon. Rush hour. Phil Stone was in the right dedicated turn lane about to turn right on a red light. Traffic was buzzing by. The marked speed limit was fifty miles per hour. Cars and trucks were all racing by, like there was a prize to win. They were pushing it hard. Phil was waiting for his chance to slip in with them. He crept forward just a little, making sure he didn't encroach on the cross traffic. As he leaned forward, looking as far left as he could see, waiting for an opening where he could merge in, it felt like a bomb went off. Phil's head snapped back. His fingers clamped down on the steering wheel. Both his knees bashed into the console. Phil had just been rear-ended.

He called 911. They asked if anyone was injured. Phil told them he was just shook up. Then they said if no one was injured in either car, he should share his insurance info with the other driver and let the insurance companies hash it out.

The lady who slammed into Phil told him how sorry she was. She was distracted by her grandkids and thought Phil had already merged. She was wrong. The back of his car was crushed, but it was still drivable. Her car had major front-end damage, but also was able to be driven. He took her information. She took his, and both of them drove off.

Phil was thinking, *"Ah. It's Friday just before five o'clock. Gotta' call Gabriel Ornstead, my insurance guy, and give him a heads-up. He's been there for me for decades. Maybe he can help steer me through this mess. Never had a car accident before."* Phil pulled Gabe's contact info up in his phone and dialed Gabe's direct line, hoping Gabe would pick up before he was off for the weekend. Just a couple of rings and a voice answered, but it was not Gabriel. It was a woman's voice—a very familiar one.

"Hi. This is Phil Stone, one of Gabriel Ornstead's customers, and I wanted to report an accident," Phil said, thinking he would be transferred to Gabe, or at least get his personal voicemail.

Instead, Phil heard, "Mr. Phil? Uh—Phil Stone?"

"Nina?" Phil was baffled. He thought, *"Did I misdial and call Nina Ross?"*

"It's me. Yes. It's Nina! You had an accident? You okay?"

"My car's not so good," Phil replied. "But I think I'm okay. Confused maybe. Don't understand how I got to you, though."

Shaking his head, trying to make sense of all this, Phil thought, *"Wow. Maybe that accident did mess me up. I do feel shaky—not quite dizzy. Not normal, that's for sure."*

Then Nina explained. "I'm here at Allworld now. I'm an Account Manager. It's amazing. When I started, I was given all of Gabe's book of residential insurance customers. I'm saying a quick 'Hi' and offering help if they need it. I'm about halfway through contacting everybody to let them know I will be taking care of them since Gabe Ornstead retired. It's alphabetical so I didn't realize your name was on it."

"Yeah. Stone," Phil said. "All through school I was always last to be called when they'd go alphabetically. Always last. Wonder what that did to my development, always being last." He chuckled. "So, you're at Allworld now?"

"Yep. Love it here. Can't wait to tell you all about it," she said. "But first—what happened to you? Tell me."

Phil gave her a quick overview of his accident, and she reassured him saying she would personally get everything handled for him. Finally, Phil could relax.

Then Nina said, "Gotta' put you on hold. Sixty seconds. Okay?" Phil agreed. Less than a minute later she was back. "Phil. It was my dad. He told me to say, 'Hi.' He asked me to pick up some ice for a little family barbecue we planned for tomorrow. Then he had an idea. You free Saturday night?"

"Uh. Yeah. What incredible timing. Just happens that Kim's at my daughter's babysitting the grandkids tomorrow evening. I'm open, but I don't want to intrude," Phil told her.

Nina laughed. "Dad said 'Get him here. Love to have him. Haven't seen him in too long. Get Phil here!' So—can we count on you?"

"Absolutely! Can't wait. Two questions: what can I bring, and what time should I plan on?"

"Seven o'clock is perfect. And bring a big appetite!"

Saturday evening Phil knocked on the door, bottle of Rombauer Chardonnay in his hand. "Phil! Come on in," Doug said as he reached for Phil's hand. "Wine? Aw. You didn't have to."

"Bet we can find something worth toasting tonight, right?" Phil answered.

Doug smiled. "Retti is the cook around here. She's out at the grill. She'll love this."

Dinner was great. Great food and great friends. The Ross family had earned a special place in Phil's heart. After the dishes were cleared and the four of them were sitting around the table, Nina stood up and gestured for Phil to stand. Nina opened her arms and hugged him saying, "I'm so thankful to you for all your help, all your guidance, and I guess mainly, that you care so much, Phil."

Phil may have been blushing when he said, "I am so proud I could have had even a minor role in your explosive career. It really has been extraordinary. You've grown into a professional. You even have the confidence and posture now to be comfortable calling me 'Phil.' I love it! Nina—you are special—impressive. You've learned at lightning speed. Tell me, what would you say is your biggest take-away on your journey to becoming a great communicator—and what's next. Where do you see yourself and your career going?"

Nina didn't hesitate. She said, "Most people are so absorbed with what is happening in their own lives, they don't think about the other person. They are locked in their own heads. The key to breaking out of that cycle is connecting with other people. The best way to connect is by asking questions. Questions are the answer!"

Phil agreed. "You are absolutely right. Questions are indeed the answer."

Nina went on. "Find out what is happening in other people's worlds, and you open up a new world of your own—for yourself. A world where you are no longer alone.

"You asked me where I want to go in my career. I don't know the 'where.' But I do know the 'what.' What I want to be is relevant. I want to make a difference—to contribute. I want to provide value. I have been blessed to have mentors who are the epitome of servant leaders. I plan on paying that forward. The things I've learned from them—and you, Phil, have changed my entire life. I believe…no…I know…I know in my heart and mind I could never have achieved so much in so little time without embracing things like alternate of choice questions or Hot Potatoes and all the dozens of techniques I've learned. I'm on my way to becoming a great communicator—and I promise to never stop—ever!"

Doug grabbed Retti's hand as they stood up, both bursting with pride, eyes bordering on tears. They raised their glasses and Doug said, "A toast. A toast to us—and to never stop—ever!"

All glasses high, in unison, the four of them pledged, "To never stop—ever!"

TOPICS FOR CONTEMPLATION AND DISCUSSION

Hey! It's me again, Phillip Stone. Welcome back to my office! Hope you enjoyed your time in Bonnerville, and are well on your way to becoming a mind reader.

Find a few powerful anti-conflict ideas and concepts? Hope so! Just in case, I've put this list together for you to review. Sorry—can't list every one of the points you could take away. There are many. Miss any? Well, here are some of the main takeaways, in the order they appear. It's stuff to think about—and talk about!

Preface: Conflict is a growing curse we must learn to control. Learn to recognize it. Learn to understand its danger. And learn to avoid it!

Chapter 1: The Magic of Choices

Events and Trends: Something happens once—it's an event. If it happens often—it's a trend. If you don't like the trend, you need to change something or live with that negative trend forever.

What's in a Name: With all people, the most important word in the world is their name. Pronounce it correctly. Use it often.

Alternate of Choice: Giving people too many options can overwhelm. Limit choices to only two at a time. Only offer choices you want chosen.

Chapter 2: Decisions

What Now moments: Life asks the question, "What now?" all the time. The effort to solve the question should be equal to the severity of the situation. Don't make a big deal about little things, and don't go into paralysis with the big ones. Keep a balance.

Good people: Surround yourself with good people and good things will follow.

Ben Franklin: Decisions can be made easier by listing the positives and the negatives in a situation. The list will help illuminate the proper path. Use this for your own decisions, and in formulating a plan to prepare for a persuasion situation.

Big ideas: Break down big ideas into small bites easily swallowed by the listener.

Conditioned Response: It's easy to avoid being sold by saying an automatic, "No!" A strong "No" gets rid of people who interrupt our moments. We develop responses to repeating situations to have control in life. When "this" happens to us—we say "that." Every time. No matter what. It becomes a habit. As with bad habits, a conditioned response is tough to control once it gets ingrained in our subconscious mind.

The power of a sincere compliment: If you spread a bunch of bull—people will surely smell it. Stay real with compliments. Use sincerity often.

Chapter 3: Acceptance

Buying a future favor: When people are thanked for their efforts, they often respond saying, "No problem." Lock in the possibility of them reciprocating by adding, "You'd do the same for me."

Celebrate your friends: They will love you for it.

Body Language: Watch closely as you talk with people. Watch everything—especially facial expressions. They say, "The eyes are the window to the soul." It's true. The look in their eyes can give you solid clues to what people are thinking.

First impressions are critical: The brain is like a computer. At lightning speed, it is evaluating, judging, deciding. You have only one chance for your first impression.

Use gradual increments: Minds can be moved easily if a big concept is broken down into smaller pieces. "How do you eat an elephant? One bite at a time."

Chapter 4: Evaluation

Investigate interest before offering options: Don't waste time and piss people off by offering choices that have zero appeal.

More hooks in the water will catch more fish: Keep as many options open as possible.

Strive for perfection: Once you get out of school, where perfect is not required, don't be satisfied with less than one hundred percent perfect. Don't accept mediocrity. Strive to hit the center of the bullseye every time. Strive!

The Silver Rule: All people have the right to be wrong. Give them space.

Murphy's Law: What can go wrong does go wrong.

Bonner's Law: What can go wrong MIGHT go wrong. If we recognize a potential negative and take action to prevent it—it won't go wrong!

Preventing a cancellation: Don't overlook telling signals, and be thorough. Can't tell you how many times I've heard a salesperson say, "I knew they might cancel." If you feel you might get a cancellation, ask the questions needed to eliminate the reason. Don't ignore the signs of an impending cancellation and do nothing but hope.

Chapter 5: Go Step-By-Step

Underpromise and Overdeliver: You will never disappoint.

Immediate gratification: People don't like to wait. Remove obstacles that cause delays. Automation can get in the way too. Watch for potential problems with your automation. Be aware of people's feelings, and use the Golden Rule.

When relating a problem to a higher-up, add a solution: When you bring problems to your manager, bring solutions too, so you are not perceived as just another whiner.

Transfer the picture in your mind to the mind of your listener: If they see things the same way you do, they will agree with you. Paint a picture in someone's mind to match the picture in yours. It's best done slowly—not abruptly—one brush stroke at a time.

Chapter 6: Perspectives

The Appropriate Apology: People will accept your apology if it is sincere and perfectly fits the situation.

Little jokes relax people: When dealing with a serious topic, don't stay serious. Relax people with humor now and then. Relaxed people will be more open to tell you their thoughts, and to accept your ideas.

Retain good talent: Why do people quit a job? Most often they feel unappreciated. Really listen to people. Show appreciation at every opportunity.

Assume the positive: Don't play Devil's Advocate searching for negatives to spotlight. Stay positive. When it's a big deal, assume the positive. Then lock in that positive with simple little questions.

Hot Potato: When you hear an ambiguous question, repeat the key words as a question. You will learn what thoughts caused their question.

Don't hard sell: People hate to be sold, but they appreciate help making a buying decision. Learn their thoughts so you can be that help.

Upselling: Always provide extra value. Whether you get more money, or simple appreciation—it is upselling. Even a simple act of kindness provides more value than was expected. It's upselling. So—upsell!

Chapter 7: Transformation

What people perceive differs: Everybody's mind works differently. With questions, find out not only what they think—but how they think.

Fear of Loss: Fear of loss is a true motivator. It lives at the heart of the world of commerce. You can use it too. It sure is used on you!

The power of a positive attitude and believing: If you believe you can't—you can't! There is no path to success without a positive attitude.

Build on positives and overcome the negatives: Don't ignore the negatives. Confront them—but gently. Nibble away at negatives while glorifying the positives.

Give your word: Then honor that commitment. Be known as being totally reliable. Be the person others can count on.

When people say "No": When people say "Yes," they can and do change their minds. But when you get a strong "No," it's tough to reverse that decision. Stop the "no" before you get it. Prevent it.

Eye contact: Critical to know what people are thinking, but eye contact can distract at the moment of the final decision. When it is time to decide, direct their total attention toward the action you want them to take.

Concentrate on the people, not what you are showing them: Learn your talk thoroughly so you can closely watch and listen to the people. If they make a funny face—you need to see it! If they make a funny sound—you need to hear it! Practice.

Every time I convince someone about anything, I have sold them: Selling is everywhere. It's just persuasion. Don't be afraid of it. Embrace it.

Chapter 8: Assumptions

Reasons why they might and might not: As you persuade others, watch for the signals that will guide you to success. Recognize reasons why they might not agree, or why they won't move in the direction you want, and tactfully overcome the negatives. Glorify the positives. Build your case on positives.

Roleplay: If you have a situation that repeats, learn the best way to deal with repeating situations by reaching for the deepest details. Pick the very best words that will make your case. Practice what you will say. If you will be talking out loud—practice out loud—not just in your mind. Remember? Practice makes...

Anger is a cry for help: We only touched on this in Bonnerville, but think about it. Can you conjure up any situation where anger would not be a cry for help?

Don't assume the best; don't assume the worst: Prepare for all likely possibilities. Avoid assumptions when you don't already know the correct answer. Don't make an *ass* out of you and *umption*.

Chapter 9: Benefits

The team is not sold yet: Team or individual, people will move to your way of thinking if they believe in your offering and clearly see the benefit to themselves and others.

Feel, Felt, Found: Formula for fantastic finishes fashioned for flourishing! Phenomenal!

Chapter 10: Challenges

Even with extensive investigation, you can miss things: Reading minds is tough when it's long distance.

Choose between point-blank and persuasion: There is a time for each. Choose wisely.

Chapter 11: Development

Avoid the arrows that threaten all pioneers: If it has never been done before, beware of the unknown. Arrows can be quite sharp.

Servant Leadership: Lift up those who work with you, at home, at work, and out in the world. Work for those who work with you. If you tell someone to jump, permit them to ask, "How high?" Don't mandate.

Timeframe—with their agreement: Tell people how long they can expect things to take. And make sure your estimate is approved and accepted by those people. Then—follow through.

Chapter 12: Mind-reading Techniques

Facts and Opinions: Choose questions that avoid the potential for conflict.

Interrogative tags: Turn statements into questions so you can learn what people are thinking by adding a simple, interrogative tag to any statement, right? Does make sense, doesn't it?

Ask how they feel about anything: However people feel, they cannot be wrong. Since there is almost no possibility of conflict, people can answer confidently without fear of being judged.

The One to Ten: People freely rate things on a one to ten because they cannot be challenged—they cannot be wrong. On a scale of one to ten, ten being the best, how likely are you to use this one-to-ten rating approach?

Get the tools you need to succeed: Don't scrimp. If you are competing with a guy driving a bulldozer, don't just bring your shovel.

The power of team: The team is your power!

Chapter 13: Elevation

Bring in the big guns: When dealing with a negative situation that requires compromise, having someone of higher authority will impress and soften the situation.

Transform negative situations into stellar events: The only time to overreact is when there is a problem. Overdo your response. Bury a negative situation with a mountain of positives. Shock them with your stellar response.

Responsibility empowers people: When people can clearly see the task, understand the objectives, and know the resulting benefits, they grow stronger and more productive—and they enjoy it!

The bigger your personality, the smaller the world gets: It's a huge world if you never leave your small cave. Get out in the world and interact. As the world shrinks, you'll find you have more access to solutions. Grow your personality—and your world, by opening yourself up to others.

All endings come with some pain: Some endings are almost totally void of pain. Almost totally. Some endings are devastating. Be ready. Anticipate.

Epilogue- *Questions are the Answer!*

Well, there you go. The end?

Nah! Not for you! First—I have a favor to ask—an easy one!

I'll bet you wish you could have joined us when Doug gave his toast, right? Go ahead. Pour a glass. Raise it and pledge: **"To never stop—ever!"**

ABOUT THE AUTHOR, BY DEBORAH GRANDINETTI, EDITOR

Now that Phillip has introduced his cast of characters and concluded his fable, I'd like to introduce the real Phillip J. Stone. I got to know him while we worked on this book together, and it's been a true pleasure! Phillip is extremely passionate about the promise of this book, which has been 20 years in the making. His aim? To equip others with the skills to create positive communications with positive outcomes—no matter what the situation. Ultimately, he envisions a more harmonious world overall, one in which people know how to talk to each other without pissing each other off.

You've probably gleaned some of Phillip's story from the book. But he was modest, so let me share some impressive facts you may not know. Phillip's first ambition to become a rock star was so strong, he left college early, took his bass guitar, and made a career in the music industry. He released three albums, one with a top regional band, Jasper Wrath; another with a band he formed, Eyes, and the third, Welcome to the Wrecking Ball, with Grace Slick, former singer and frontwoman of Jefferson Airplane. As he mentions in the book, Welcome to the Wrecking Ball hit number forty-nine on the Billboard international charts in 1981. Then Phillip made a dramatic turn, as you learned in

Chapter 7. He went into the home alarm business with his dad. What he doesn't tell you in the book is that he and his dad made the business so successful, it became the number #1 franchise of over 200 franchises in the alarm industry. Those were the years Phillip went all in, studying everything he could and testing and refining his skills to master the art of persuasion. Phillip's persuasion skills served him so well in network marketing, part-time he earned a strong five-figure check each month. His skills also helped him bring tremendous value to a large manufacturer in the home improvement industry based in Tampa, Florida. When the time was right, Phillip was instrumental in packaging the company for a $92 Million sale!

www.ingramcontent.com/pod-product-compliance
Lightning Source LLC
Chambersburg PA
CBHW020459030426
42337CB00011B/160